A Good Enough Story i that God has done in S God's heart for each of biblical concepts. Sara's story calls us to see each of our stories in light of the gospel of grace, and bids us to grasp who God says we are and walk into all He's created us to be.

Rev. Dr. Daniel Zopoula
Author, Lead Pastor of The Miz City Church,
CEO of Bridges of Hope
daniel@themizcitychurch.org
www.mizcitychurch.com
www.thebridgesofhope.com

Some scars are visible and present for the world to see. Most scars are hidden deep within us as we pretend we are okay. Sara shows us both in this hard journey of discovering of who she really is in light of God and His grace. Her poetic prose and heartfelt writing of childhood angst and bullying touches the heart of every person who remembers their own past. Where most of us find our footing, Sara goes deeper into her own mind of perfection and failure, becoming her own judge and jury. God walks beside Sara through it all, never giving up on her. You won't put this book down until you walk through the victory with her. I pray this book helps us to ask more questions, listen more, pray mightily, and be there for children and adults that may struggle with these same issues.

Phylis Mantelli
Author, Motivational Speaker, Life Coach
phylismantelli05@gmail.com
www.phylismantelli.com

Dear Karen,

To God be the glory – great things He has done!

And great are the things He continues to do!

May you know the fullness of love God has for you in Jesus Christ.

(Ephesians 3:16-21)

♡
Sara Kennerley

A GOOD ENOUGH *Story*

SARA KENNERLEY

A GOOD ENOUGH STORY
Copyright © 2021 by Sara Kennerley

All rights reserved. Neither this publication nor any part of this publication may be reproduced or transmitted in any form or by any means, electronic or mechanical, including photocopying, recording or any information storage and retrieval system, without permission in writing from the author.

Scripture quotations marked (ESV) are from the ESV® Bible (The Holy Bible, English Standard Version®), copyright © 2001 by Crossway, a publishing ministry of Good News Publishers. Used by permission. All rights reserved. Scripture quotations marked (NLT) are taken from the Holy Bible, New Living Translation, copyright ©1996, 2004, 2015 by Tyndale House Foundation. Used by permission of Tyndale House Publishers, a Division of Tyndale House Ministries, Carol Stream, Illinois 60188. All rights reserved. Scripture quotations taken from the Amplified® Bible (AMP), Copyright © 2015 by The Lockman Foundation. Used by permission. www.Lockman.org. Scripture quotations marked (NIV) are taken from the Holy Bible, New International Version®, NIV®. Copyright © 1973, 1978, 1984, 2011 by Biblica, Inc.® Used by permission of Zondervan. All rights reserved worldwide. www.zondervan.com The "NIV" and "New International Version" are trademarks registered in the United States Patent and Trademark Office by Biblica, Inc.® Scripture marked (NKJV) taken from the New King James Version®. Copyright © 1982 by Thomas Nelson. Used by permission. All rights reserved.

ISBN: 978-1-4866-2082-1
eBook ISBN: 978-1-4866-2083-8

Printed in Canada

Word Alive Press
119 De Baets Street Winnipeg, MB R2J 3R9
www.wordalivepress.ca

Cataloguing in Publication information can be obtained from Library and Archives Canada.

Contents

Introduction	vii
Prologue	xi
One: Elementary School	1
Two: Middle School	7
Three: High School	13
Four: The Slippery Slope	19
Five: The Hard Crash	25
Six: More Bitter Brokenness	33
Seven: A Grace-filled Introduction	39
Eight: The Encounter with Mercy	45
Nine: The Bumpy, Redeemed Road	51
Ten: God-Breathed Embraces, Forged from the Ashes	57
Eleven: The Fibromyalgia Roadblock	65
Twelve: The Farse of Perfection in Motherhood	71
Thirteen: Hope for the Not-Quites	77
Fourteen: New Life, New Name!	85
Fifteen: Grace, Grace, and More Grace	91
Sixteen: Living Good Enough	97
After Thoughts	101

Introduction

As I reflect on my juvenile years, a few key themes stand out to me: relationships, school, and athletics. Interwoven in each was my faith, which pushed me towards excellence. My intent was good. I was aiming for joy by loving God and others as myself, to the best of my capacity.

Along the way, though, I missed the mark.

Individually, the memories I share may not have huge significance, and truthfully they would not be considered "traumatic," yet they have played a role in shaping my character. My hope is that they point to how easily common and normal childhood experiences can turn harmful if they aren't directed and processed appropriately.

In my own story, this did indeed prove to be true. For ten dark years of my young adult life, I felt defeated and hopeless. I didn't date, work, or finish university. Neither did I travel to see the world. I barely stayed alive, but for God's grace.

Reflecting on these memories feels bittersweet. A part of me often wishes to go back and change things to avoid the path I ended up taking. Another part of me grieves the years of my life that I lost—years that could have been spent thriving, advancing with sprightly steps out towards the bright horizon ahead.

But there is no reset button. There is only grace, and the choice to trust that God's work of redemption is so much better than anything

I could accomplish on my own. The faith I had as a child is different than the faith I now have, and that makes sense. It's a sign that I am growing and learning, even with the stumbles I've made along the way.

When I felt God nudge me to write my story back in 2018, I had the book title in mind, but I had no idea how the story would unfold. Today, looking at the finished manuscript, I can truly sit back and stand in awe of the beautiful way God has walked me through this whole writing journey.

This book, *my* good enough story, wouldn't be complete without the poetry that's dispersed through each chapter. I've always loved poetry and I wish I still had the poetry journals I wrote in my youth. Still, I stand firm in God's faithfulness, He makes all things new!

The poetry tale of "A Princess in Abba's Kingdom" was inspired by my writing group, another one of those delightfully brilliant gifts from God. The women there lit a fire in me to keep writing poetry, for in it they saw my heart and my voice come alive.

Well, late one night I had a vision of the perfect poetry piece for my book: a fairy tale of a princess who mirrors my earthly story and champions faith, hope, and love for Abba! Had I left it there, I'd have been so happy with how the poetry turned out. But while chatting with a dear friend one night, after she'd been a beta reader of this book, she commented on the symbolism I'd totally missed—the princess is me, of course, and globally we are all princesses and princes in Abba's Kingdom.

Yet it goes deeper. My name, Sara, actually means "princess." This was something I'd totally skipped over in the visionary stage, but when my friend mentioned it I was floored by the realization! In a later chapter, I delve into the meaning of names and labels, and yet I'd not seen this correlation myself while penning the poem. It takes the beauty of the imagery to a whole new level for me.

As I continue walking out my good enough story, I choose to define myself as Beloved of God rather than Not Quite, which so tore apart my soul. And as a fairy tale princess, I can live in a heavenly way, fixing my eyes on what is unseen rather than what is seen (2 Corinthians 4:18) in this epic saga with the ultimate happily-ever-after ending… all thanks to God's grace.

This realization brings a smile to my face, as I hope it does to yours, too. Be blessed in the reading, friends.

SARA KENNERLEY

Once upon a time, in a land not so far away
There lived a Princess…

A sweet little girl
With a spring in her step and a song in her heart

She was the delight of her Abba
The King

Eyes shining
Reflecting the light of Abba's presence
She skipped about her days

Inhaling
The abundance of Abba's good gifts

A basket in hand
She was off to gather flowers for a lovely bouquet…

Prologue

I'd danced in this Sunday school classroom for preschoolers countless times. The warmth of the smiles that greeted me made my heart soar with excitement. The brightly coloured wall art captivated my desires to be and to create. This room, this place, was love.

The circle of equally sunshiney faces joined me, wide-eyed, as we stared up at our teacher. Together we recited our daily prayer. Jesus, this mysterious man from long ago who sparked such love, such happiness in my days, He could hear me talking to Him? The concept was beyond fathoming, and yet I embraced it. This day's prayer settled deep in my being, and silently I asked Jesus to make His home in my heart, to be my new best friend.

Time now for some music. The teacher turned the volume up, and we danced blissfully. Our Sunday school dresses twirled with poetic precision. Our ponytails caught the breeze of our tipsy pirouttés and ushered us into merriment. We sang as we spun, and sometimes focused long enough to enact the gestures the teacher was showing us to aid in the memorization of the lyrics—silly words of stories from a faraway land, a faraway time: Noah and an ark, Abraham and his son Isaac, Joseph and his multicoloured coat, and angels in the sky above a town called Bethlehem.

Mixed with the giggles of the friends who surrounded me, I felt settled, content in this remarkable world of faith, love, and Jesus. Ushered into our next activity, I grinned with anticipation.

With my legs crossed, elbows rested sharply on my knees, I stared up at the lesson of the day on the corkboard: JOY. The colourful block letters jumped off their mount and swooned in my mind. That day I learned that JOY stood for *Jesus, Others, Yourself*. To have a joy-filled life, this is the order of purpose to pursue. And like a fuzzy-ended piece of Velcro on my sticky-ended brain, the lesson attached itself to me...

A GOOD ENOUGH STORY

SARA KENNERLEY

The field up ahead beckoned her
The excitement
The wonder

A rainbow of swaying petals
Glittered the expanse

Her feet felt light as air
Her gaze fixed
That rainbow
Her favourite treat gifted by Abba so far

Her fingertips itched
To dust across the delicate masterpiece
Of flowers dancing along
To the songs of heaven

Then suddenly
THUD

One:
Elementary School

I was a bright child, drawn in by the fascination of learning. The world was a wonder-filled place, my appetite whetted by the lessons fed me throughout preschool, kindergarten, early grade school, and Sunday school.

During these primal years, my parents enrolled me in our local church's Awana program, which teaches Bible memorization and awards badges. The competition and recognition of excellence offered at Awana fuelled me to achieve more and more.

My childhood was a seesaw adventure, balancing the excitement of singing songs at church while aspiring to the moral code of the Bible verses I memorized as I applied myself to the growing demands of excellence.

But these questions in particular hung heavily over me. Am I giving Jesus and others enough? Have I given well enough?

I loved sport and from an early age was motivated by athletics. I was persistent and determined and pushed to reach the limits set before me. My parents gave me ample opportunities to enjoy sports, too. I played softball as a tyke and loved the thrill of running bases and defeating the field team with my speed and fearless drive. I couldn't hit the ball very well, but I bravely stood my ground at home base and eagerly took wildly thrown balls so I could get on base. What's a momentary smack of pain, or a bruise, if it provides the chance to get in the game and make an impact, right?

While out in the field, I was my team's star shortstop. I loved this position, which gave me free rein to snag the balls before they could make it to the outfield. Unafraid, I met those balls, poised and impassioned.

I believe it was the social aspect of the game, rather than the sport itself, which ultimately drew me away from softball. My best friend turned enemy, Eden, was a peer on the ball diamond. When our friendship ended, so too did my engagement with softball.

Friendships were intimidating. I longed to make heartfelt and significant connections with others, but instead I was met with much rejection and bullying.

Eden towered over me by a foot. Her dark hair cascaded over her strong jaw and caught the eyes of every other child on the schoolyard. She was a playmate and friend, until it no longer suited her interests.

The turning point in our friendship is one I honestly can't remember with much clarity. I believe it centred around a cookie I had brought as a snack one day. I chose to eat it in its entirety rather than share with her. What should have been an insignificant moment between two friends at recess ended up becoming a defining moment of bitterness.

Eden became a constant threat to me. A troop of "chimpanzees," her followers/friends, marched around her at all times. Almost overnight, it seemed, she grew into one of the most popular girls around. She was a confident leader and demanded the respect of the masses. They pointed their fingers whenever they spotted me, laughing at my attempts to simply "be." Was their laughter warranted? Was I a ridiculous creature? The answer was unclear, or at least up for internal debate.

Miraculously, my faith came alive during these years of scorn. I began to walk with the lonely and rejected. My eyes saw their pain, and side by side we stood stronger, dodging spitballs and flaming words meant to destroy us.

Emsley was one such companion. Mousy-haired and rather slovenly, hers was a heart that understood exclusion. But she had the spirit of a swan and the motivation of a ravenous lion to live and love.

She experienced rejection like no one else I witnessed in my early life. On a shallow level, I understood and saw the differences that made her stand apart from the crowd. I was drawn deeper into friendship, though, despite her awkward appearance, likely because of the rooted faith developing in my heart.

After being tossed aside by Eden like a fast food wrapper, I opened my arms to Emsley and shared my school days with her. We walked the schoolyard at recess, just the two of us, chattering about little girl silliness. But the targets on our backs, Emsley's most of all, were flashing signs that drew in the bullies, ready to pounce. At intervals, the ungracious little chimpanzees would approach us, bent on showering us with their spit. Literally.

I'll never know how painful those moments were for Emsley. I believe that God allowed my own rejection to come at an early age, though, to help Emsley walk through her pain and hopefully come out the other side with faith and confidence.

Emsley taught me how to serve in love, how to humbly choose disgrace in the eyes of the world and therein find a blessing. My nagging debate over my own worth seemed to die down when I fixed my eyes on loving this rejected outcast beside me.

Getting chastised was horribly painful for me, too intense an experience to be kissed better and covered with a cute Band-Aid. It seared deep, attacking my identity as someone who strived to be perfect and live according to the black and white rules I understood. It stamped me with the ugly word "failure."

While in the second grade, I decided one day that my time in the library had ended too soon. The bell rang just as the stories were coming alive, and my cozy corner begged me to grab a couple more titles and indulge myself. The problem is that I had to get to music class. That day, my love of the library's peaceful solitude trumped everything, so I chose to ignore the bell and stay hidden in my corner of the library to read.

Unfortunately, it wasn't long before my music teacher was staring me down with a scowl. Heart racing, legs weak and shaky, she coerced me into standing up in front of my peers and declaring a heartfelt apology for my heinous crime. My shame was like bile in my throat, and my voice wobbled as I delivered the apology.

Every ounce of my being told me that from that point on, I would do all that my teachers asked of me—and I did exactly that, embracing my peer-awarded title: teacher's pet. I wore this badge fervently for the rest of my school days. No other labels afforded me the same comfort to learn and thrive—so I embraced it, despite the teasing.

In Grade Four, we had thirty desks in our classroom, minus the teacher's… and twenty-nine of them held clowns. Clowns who united in a force of chaos to overthrow the teacher, a man of authority and insight. What lessons could be learned when the room was full of airborne erasers and paper balls? What insight could be absorbed when a chorus of laughter and retorts banged incessantly against my ears?

The chaos caused me deep heartache. I felt helpless against it. My classmates' disrespect fuelled a battle within my spirit to seek after what was right. Even if they themselves were fine with their choices and actions, I wasn't. But what could I do with this righteous anger?

Tears fogged my vision at the witness of my teacher's loss of control. He had to have been a man marked by troubled thoughts and a troubled spirit—how else could he fail so miserably at holding these young clowns in order?

But I was not meant to be a victorious heroine in this classic story of injustice.

My fourth-grade teacher's failures made me feel insignificant in my desire to uphold integrity in the world and helpless to resolve the torment I witnessed around me.

I now had two years left in elementary school—two years of focused academic effort and a growing timidity of spirit. Jesus still caught my young affections, and together we walked hand in hand toward the impending transition to middle school.

A GOOD ENOUGH STORY

Dirt and pebbles grazed her palms
Scraping flesh and ushering tears

Startled
The Princess looked down at the path beneath her
An unanticipated dip
That'd sent her tumbling

Persistent care and attention
Would now mingle with joyous occasions
Such as picking precious wildflowers
From Abba's exquisite field

Fumbling at first, she found it
The tinker of her glass jar nestled safe inside her satchel
Brought a smile

Brushing the tears from her cheeks
She cautiously dropped them, one at a time,
Into the confines of the glass treasure

The jar, an intricate piece,
A baby dedication present
From Abba

His promise to her:
Every
Tear
Mattered

Two:

Middle School

My love for sport didn't die even after leaving softball, so I dove into competitive swimming. My mom had taken me swimming consistently since I was six months old. It got her out of the house as a young mom and breathed into me a love of water. By the age of ten, I had earned all the swim lesson badges that were available.

The water kept calling, though, and I kept answering with the enthusiasm of a dolphin, ready to splash and play. It greeted me with a warm embrace, and I returned its friendship with keen interest and motivation. I studied swimming techniques—kicking harder, diving farther, and gliding faster—all to achieve the next prize: a provincial medal. After that success, who knew? Maybe I'd represent Canada at the Olympics one day! It was a glowing dream, the passionate heart cry of a prepubescent girl with the whole world at her fingertips.

Through hours of training and many weekends spent at swim meets, I learned that my true gifting was endurance swimming. Pair me against an opponent for a quick sprint and I'd likely I'd lose, but drop me in a long race and I would endure to the end and finish strong. I stood taller and prouder as I reflected on the strength this required.

That is, until my strength was attacked. While making a flip-turn off the pool wall in practice one day, I felt a sharp pain in my lower back—and just like that, my dream of competitive swimming was over. What exactly had happened? I never did find out. But the pain took my breath away in that moment.

Finishing that lap was hard—and every lap after it would be, too. My every kick was passionate and proud, but my body ached, my back weakened. Everyday childhood duties felt like taxing blows, but I endured.

My new friend was a soothing menthol cream that remained at the edge of the pool deck. It met me with a cool kiss every time I heaved my anguished body out of the pool. Its fragrance was enticing, like freshly baked peanut butter cookies. After the sensual encounter, I'd roll onto my back to stretch and rest. It was my new rhythm and routine.

A big provincial tournament was on the horizon, and I was still going to try for it. The pain would simply have to take a back seat.

When the day finally arrived, I stepped into the enormous pool arena with excitement. I had qualified for a few different events, but I had only one main focus: the race that would earn me my prize, the eight-hundred-meter. It was the longest event someone my size and gender could enter. I could taste victory.

The official's gun went off and I met the water with a skilled dive, then fell into my determined rhythm. I spotted my competitors through my goggles as we continued back and forth, the sight of their shadows pushing me into overdrive. My legs kicked harder, faster. My arms scooped the water with force and intention. When my body signalled for me to breathe and coast, I ignored it. As I approached each flip-turn, I counted down the remaining laps; the lower the numbers got, the harder I pushed myself.

The end was in sight, the glory to come worth every second of the prolonged physical ordeal. As I approached the finish, I reached my hand to edge of the pool to stop the timer. Looking up, breathless, I saw that three other girls had made it just ahead of me. I'd come in fourth place, one spot away from a medal.

It was a gut-wrenching conclusion, given that I'd known this would be my last moment to shine in competitive swimming. I'd already decided I'd be throwing in the towel after this meet.

Despite all the congratulations—fourth place in the whole province is, of course, a wonderful accomplishment—the ugliness of defeat ate away at me. I hated myself for coming so close and yet finishing so far behind.

And the pain? It would only increase and continue to weaken me. Day by day, whether sitting or standing or lying down, it was all painful. Nothing felt easy anymore.

As I progressed beyond the childhood phase of strictly memorizing Bible verses, I began to understand what was I was reading. The red letters in Matthew 5:48 beckoned me to rise even higher: *"You therefore must be perfect, as your heavenly Father is perfect"* (ESV). Challenge accepted. These words came from Jesus, my first love. What more was there to know or understand than His exact words staring up at me?

To be perfect was now the ultimate goal, and I clung to that aspiration.

Continuing through school, I focused on grades with laser-like focus. Anything less than a hundred percent wouldn't suffice. It was like bitterness to my teenage lips.

"Oh, wow!" my dad would exclaim teasingly. "You got ninety-eight percent! Where did you go wrong?"

Externally, I laughed along with him, happy to know I was accepted and praised for doing well. Internally, though, that missing two percent screamed at me and flagged me as incompetent.

The introduction of bonus points was an intriguing concept. When I discovered I had the opportunity to score one hundred and five percent? Well now, that was a challenge worth tackling! However, even one hundred percent now looked pitiable. If above perfect was attainable, perfect was no longer good enough.

Relationally, navigating through adolescence was a challenge for me. Eden and her chimpanzees carried on into middle school, growing their community of bullying, mindless beasts.

I felt the pull to hide away like a tortoise, too scared to join the band, too scared to join the choir. These extracurricular programs created a tightly knit bond of classmates I would have loved being a part of, not to mention the fun of the activities themselves. But instead

I chose art classes, which allowed me to sit alone, to dive further into my own mind and create. Or at least try to create. Creativity is highly subjective, which was my struggle. I never felt like a success in that class, and my attempts to create something beautiful from nothing always felt like they'd fallen short.

At the start of Grade Nine, my dad announced that he had accepted a pastoring position in an entirely new city. The idea of moving was a welcome thought at first. I felt a bit sad to leave my home and the people I knew, but I was also excited by the idea of starting fresh.

The excitement lingered... until I actually stepped foot on the campus of my new school. I don't think I fully realized how hard it would be to make new friends in my last year of middle school, at a time when my classmates' friendships and cliques were already long-established. I struggled to find my niche in this sea of brand-new faces. The hallways between classrooms ignited terror, motivating me to sprint rather than saunter as most did.

I did reach out to a few girls, though, who welcomed me into a network of average-type teens. Not long into my engagement with this clique of girls, while still studying them to see how I might best align myself, the group had a falling out. The details escape me, though young girls are good at having falling outs for no significant reason.

When the dust settled, a girl named Chelsey was left sitting alone, rejected and likely with a bruised heart. She was my girl. I latched onto her and the two of us finished off Grade Nine together, happier knowing that we mattered—that we belonged, at least to each other.

She and I attended a local youth group and applied our hearts to its studies and activities. It was a fun time. A busy time. My eyes were opened up to many new ideas and situations—boys, weekend youth retreats, worship, bucketball.[1]

I craved the physical impact of a bucketball game. Slam me to the ground, and I'd get back up and slam you down. Trip me, and I'd

---

[1] Bucketball had no real rules, per se. It was played on an open field and the object was to get your ball into the bucket, usually a garbage bin, by whatever means necessary. It was violent but fun. While researching the game now, I've found a completely different game by the same name, so it may not have ever been a documented "sport."

chase you down, steal the ball, and score on you. Chelsey and I were usually the only two girls on the field; the rest were boys. We loved the uniqueness and attention this brought. We were tough, just like the guys.

I still remember the first concert I attended—Newsboys, from their *Going Public* album. It was amazing. From the other youth retreats and conferences I was blessed to attend, I also remember seeing Michael W. Smith live. My heart soared when he sat at his piano. I imagined choirs of angels in attendance as our multitude of waving hands filled the air echoing praise of our God and Creator.

My youth pastor, Brenton, saw spiritual gifts in me and gave me opportunities to grow into them. Multiple times he asked me to write Bible study lessons. He would review them but they were my words to present, my passion to indulge and teach.

He also opened my eyes to less black-and-white thinking in the church. Certain movies and music which were off-limits at home and in the fundamental Baptist community I'd been raised in could be consumed here, and discerned individually. I didn't really embrace this. I often sat uncomfortably through movies and topics I felt weren't right.

But overall, I liked the idea of the community that was growing around me, despite the different points of view we held.

My middle school had been challenging, my inner turmoil growing, but I purposed to live fully alive in my faith and step forward into all I could achieve and accomplish along the way.

High school felt like another fresh opportunity to make a lasting and powerful impact in the world.

Tears stored
Safe and secure
The sting of pain still remained

Her hands cried out
Her foot throbbed too
Echoing the elevated tempo of her beating heart

Her dress
Wrinkled
Her hair
Flying away in wisps

But her cautious, slow steps
Still carried her to the anticipated beauty ahead

She marvelled at the expanse
Denying the throbbing pain for a time.
Purposing herself to her task
Choosing a thankful heart

The predicted beauty did not disappoint
And a stunning collection of flowers grew
Delicately adorning the intricate weaves of her basket
Like sapphires on a crown of gold

Smile widening, her resolve grew
Pressing on, the pain that stifled her innocence
Faded
But only for a short time…

Three:

High School

Chelsey and I bonded tightly as we walked into our new high school, preparing to finish off these last years of school with confidence and ease. I felt like part of a crowd, hanging out at her locker between classes. She drew others to her, especially boys.

Soon Chelsey began dating different guys who had previously been youth group friends, and this caught me off-guard. I suddenly felt like a third wheel and became flooded with loneliness once more.

I studied the interactions between Chelsey and each of the boys who courted her. I didn't understand any of it. Maybe it was because I had embraced my dad's household rule—"My daughter will not date until she is sixteen." Or maybe I was simply odd. But dating situations seemed dumb to me. Disgusting even. I wanted nothing to do with them. I just wanted my friend back—the girl who made me feel brave, alive, and free.

After setting aside my funk, I was thankful for the Christian club on our high school campus. I chose to invest myself in the search for a like-minded friend there and engaged in the lunchtime networking. With each day of this focused pursuit of friendship, Chelsey faded further away into her circle of boys and alcohol.

One day, when reaching out to the campus's Christian youth leader, he scolded me for choosing to walk away from Chelsey. His words shattered my spirit.

"That was a very un-Christian decision you made, Sara," he began. "You should have stayed by Chelsey's side and directed her away from the temptation she was walking into. Instead you abandoned her."

"But I was lonely and uncomfortable. I needed to let go and move on."

"Well, what does that say about your love for her?"

Sigh. Silence.

I nodded and retreated into my own world of bitter defeat.

Even though his words likely held a mixture of truth and his own opinion and emotion, all I heard was the judgment. I was unable to separate the wheat from the chaff.

I couldn't let go of this sting of failure. I'd failed Chelsey, and I'd failed Jesus and His gospel message. How utterly loathsome.

Still, I pressed on. I met a new friend, Ashley, whose passion and love for Jesus inspired and encouraged me. Ashley had grown up in the church and spent many summers at camp. She loved worship, could play the guitar, and sang like the heavenly angels she reminded me of. She was a gift. I attached myself to her with all that I had left inside me. I needed her.

While most young people my age stayed up late listening to music or hanging out with friends, I kept a steady bedtime routine and rhythm, crashing into an exhausted heap on my bed by eight o'clock. The relentless drone of my alarm clock would wake me at 5:30 a.m. every morning. I'd reach over to the nightstand for my book and journal to begin my day on the right foot. Books like *I Kissed Dating Goodbye* by Joshua Harris and *Jesus Freaks* by DC Talk were my morning caffeine. The words jumped off the page and settled in my spirit, calling me to a deeper commitment to Jesus and a more explicit expression of my faith.

Though outwardly I lived the life of a passionate Jesus Freak, inwardly I was spent. I was scared to move, in case I made the wrong move. I was falling apart yet still desperate to hold fast and succeed.

Every morning, I arrived at school early to deliver treats and handwritten notes of encouragement to the teachers' mailboxes. The notes were random, short, and sweet—intended to bless them and spread hope and joy into the school's atmosphere.

I attended to those mailboxes religiously. The teachers were a vital ministry to me, more than my peers. My peers were more terrifying to relate to and understand, but I still tried.

In English class one day, we were given an assignment to create a dream board. It was a fun project that allowed for creativity and self-expression. The dream board was supposed to be a poster-sized collage that spoke to where we saw ourselves in the years ahead. What did we want to do? Who did we want to be? Where did we want to go? When the board was complete, our next task was to present it to our classmates, to explain our choices and processes.

My dream board had a Jesus fish at the centre, cut from construction paper, brightly contrasted against the rest of the board's magazine clippings. I boldly told my classmates that I had intentionally placed Jesus at the centre because no matter what other dreams and goals I had, He—and my faith in Him—was at the centre.

I honestly have no idea whether my speech was well received, but I remember the students teasing me in that classroom many times, calling me a teacher's pet. But it would be nice to know if my proclamation did plant a seed in someone's heart.

My English teacher was another impactful person in my life. Miss J was young and confident and her spirit attracted me.

One day after class, I approached her desk and asked if she would be interested in being a mentor to me. I was struggling so hard to excel—not in her classroom, per se, but at life in general—and I was drawn to the idea of her as a mentor/big sister.

She agreed, and I later found out that she too was a Christian. We spent hours outside of the classroom, more so after she was no longer my teacher. We went for walks and shopped together. I'd barf out all the garbage that was eating me up inside and she'd comfort me and direct me to let it go.

"Let it roll off your back, Sara," she would often say.

Like a duck whose feathers are oiled to prevent them from becoming waterlogged, I needed to apply a layer of oil to my own heart and mind so life's attacks and pains didn't weigh me down.

What exactly was the *oil* that a person could tangibly apply? It was nothing that could be bought at a store, this I knew. It was the ability to guard my heart from that which aimed to destroy me. It felt like a hopeless endeavour to try and master this skill.

I longed to walk as confidently as Miss J did, but I was swimming against the current, already feeling the weight of water pulling me down and threatening to sink me.

What had happened to joy and the promise of its presence from that Sunday school lesson in my childhood? Behind all the striving, all the relentless focus to get everything right, I was still counting on that promised but foreign destination of a joy-filled life. Where was it? Certainly I had given all of myself. Joy was nowhere in sight.

I remember spending many lunch breaks and free periods sitting alone in the corner of my school's halls. I searched out and found many favourite spots to escape to. There, I clung to my Bible and my journal, and studiously reflecting on how to get myself unstuck from the mire of weighty emotions bogging me down.

One of my high school teachers applied an interesting technique to his classroom: he had a teddy bear that was free grabs to anyone who wasn't feeling able to engage with the class on any given day. The teddy could sit on top of a student's desk and be a pass for them, as long as they physically remained in attendance. I exchanged many an embrace with that teddy over the course of the term. The teddy even caught some of my well-smothered tears on days when the pressure overwhelmed me.

The last two years of classes were hard. So hard. Math was the bane of my existence. Chemistry and physics were easily tossed aside and replaced with language studies like Spanish and German. But math, it was a necessary evil that I had to endure and excel in even though I despised it. I tackled tests and assignments with woe-filled toiling, weary yet aware of the master's approaching whip.

I graduated high school fourth in my class of over three hundred students.[2] Though not the valedictorian, I was asked to present the induction speech. What an honour! A terrifying honour! What was I to say to encourage the nearly one thousand faces gazing up from the chairs in front of me? This was my ultimate moment to have an impact on my peers and the people celebrating with them.

I attacked this final school mission with valour. I prepared a well-crafted metaphor to inspire and delight my listeners. It was a lyrical beauty. Perfection. That I had to be the one to present it, though… well, that just felt wrong.

On the day of the ceremony, my voice reeked of anxiety. My knees trembled as I clung to the podium.

But the cordial applause still came.

Afterward I returned to my seat and continued along with the program set before me, ending the chapter of my youth and preparing for the immense undertaking that would come next: postsecondary education and the checklist I'd established for becoming a successful adult.

These were heavy weights, yet I remained fixated on the dreams and accomplishments that were mine to pursue.

My first love and best friend, Jesus, remained by my side, but my eyes had become glazed over with too many distortions and false glories to see the true beauty of His heart for me. I couldn't understand my innate worth.

---

[2] Another fourth place finish… I wonder if that was just a coincidence, or maybe a deeper connection in my story?

Purple petals popped
From behind a cove of yellow

The Princess purposed over
Dreaming once more of the bouquet to come.

Reaching down to pluck the specimen
Another stabbing searing
Rush of PAIN!

This time
Her already battered palms
Bitterly screamed in anger

The Princess nearly broke
At the sight of the jagged array

Thorns
Standing on edge across her hand's expanse
Like tiny soldiers of torture

Four:
The Slippery Slope

My seventeen-year-old eyes bravely took in the campus, much larger than anything I'd experienced before. I was an immigrant in a new land.

Gulping down anxiety, hands clenched tight, I stepped ahead into this overwhelming world. The giants who surrounded me were indeed terrifying creatures, sharply tailored and echoing confident babble that my ears strained to understand. I was a grasshopper fit to be trampled or consumed, but a grasshopper still determined to arrive at my goal: a bachelor of arts in psychology, my stepping stone to a master's degree in speech and language pathology.

My backpack carried twenty pounds of textbooks, and twenty more of fear—that I would be devoured by this crazy world. I affixed a smile to my face as with a glue stick and screamed, *This is me! Please don't eat me! Love me, and walk with me!*

The evaluation processes in this new world were so foreign and aggravating. How could I work ten times harder than in high school and receive grades that were ten percent lower? I simply wasn't going to make it.

As hard as I tried, my anxiety only grew. The stinging pain of failure, or what felt like failure, was getting to be too much.

I became an expert at camouflaging myself in the hallways of this new campus. Like a flaming tree longing for rain, my spirit cried out for relief.

I found that relief, though not in an anticipated form. A classmate inadvertently introduced me to the art of self-harm one afternoon in the middle of a lecture. Pausing from the hum of nonsense being directed at me from the front of the room, I spotted a "fellow immigrant" with raw wounds on her wrist. This was an odd vision, like nothing I had witnessed in life. But it sent me deeper in a quest to quiet the raging fire of disappointing failure.

After that day's tiresome lecture, I reached out to my new friend, whose name now escapes me, and later heard more about the rationale behind the wounds, as well as her techniques for inflicting them. How very inspiring a thought it was to release the rage from within and let it seep out of my flesh so I could continue to live and breathe this noxious foreign air.

The first instrument of self-harm I wielded was a pen. Amidst the continuing nonsensical hum of daily lectures, its lid dug deeper into the skin of my wrist. I was amazed at how inconspicuously this could be achieved. It also drove me to question, *Are these giants around me really so dense and blind to the plights of grasshoppers that self-inflicted violence can go completely unnoticed?*

Perhaps it actually was noticed, but laughed off as a stupid grasshopper trait. Either way, it was freeing indeed. The raging fire within my spirit did seem to die down briefly, a welcome relief.

Where was my Jesus, you may ask yourself? Why wouldn't I give Him my anxieties and inner turmoil? Surely by now I'd studied the Scriptures enough to know what they say about *"casting all your care upon Him, for He cares for you"* (1 Peter 5:7, NKJV). Jesus, my Jesus, also says, *"My yoke is easy and My burden is light"* (Matthew 11:30, NKJV).

If He had been my first love and passion throughout my youth, how could I let myself slip away into such dark territory?

If my story is starting to sound all too familiar to you, oh my heart hurts for you.

For the first few months of my dangerous university trek, I lived at home with my parents in order to save money. Unfortunately, my dad was walking through his own brokenness around this time, which created a complicated relationship and home environment. For years he had embraced the call to study God's Word and pastor churches. But the ugliness of church politics marked the end of an era for my dad. It was a bitter, startlingly bitter, hurt that nearly broke him. The vipers had struck at an evening board meeting, at which I'd been taking the minutes as an act of service and support. My memories of that night are a distant blur.

Leaving the meeting that night, my dad drove me home and later took himself for a ride to process what had happened alone. Overcome by the turmoil he'd just endured, and engaged in a battle with depression, he literally contemplated driving himself off the road. Where was God? Certainly not in the venomous words of his fellow churchgoers.

Not only did he leave the church after this awful blow, both as a leader and as an attendee, but he sought refuge in the numbing company of alcohol. And herein lay the root of our severed relationship, adding much woe between us over the next few years.

I reached out to a youth pastor who offered me the opportunity to be a live-in nanny rent-free while continuing my education. What a blessing this was! The love I received from this family's two small boys surpassed anything my heart could fathom. Their joy for life, their giggles and snuggles, were my sustenance and nourishment when the rest of the world made no sense.

If only those two sweet boys' love could have satisfied me longer-term. Alas, my heart had tasted the bitter fruit of self-harm, which soon erupted into even darker, more penetrating ugliness.

I was sinking, fast—consumed by this dreaded world that I'd worked so hard to overcome despite my grasshopper status. Three semesters into my university career, I sought help from a campus counsellor. A kitchen sink could not have contained the tears that had already fallen from my broken heart, nor could an ocean reach the depths of my pain. This counsellor didn't stand a chance of reaching me and making a difference.

Instead she was the voice that advised, "Give up. Pack your bags and emigrate elsewhere. Grasshoppers can't survive in this world." And so I did.

After only a few months of dragging a pen across my flesh, its benefits were less than satisfactory. I quickly advanced into cutting my flesh with knives. It didn't take long before the beloved family I lived with discovered this secret. One cold, gloomy day, I was kindly asked to leave. Knives and open wounds had no place around sweet innocent boys. Painfully, I knew this to be true, but my spirit saw no other place for relief.

A GOOD ENOUGH STORY

Steadfastness scoffed
The Princess succumbed to the torturous thorns
Each pain-filled pull to un-station a soldier
Aroused agony, uncontained.

Her wailing interrupted the songs of heaven around her
Her tears puddled
Her heart broke

How could her glass jar collect and contain
This surplus spill of sadness
And pain.

She didn't even bother to search for and try to open it.

Five:

The Hard Crash

Onward and downward. I was now the newest resident at a local group home for at-risk community members. The compounding failures were stacking all the way to heaven, banging on the entrance and screaming at God, *Why do You hate? I gave everything for You! I tried and tried and tried. Was I not good enough? I will never be good enough for You!*

There was nothing left—no need for God, no need for faith, no need for pursuing a meaningful life whatsoever. The downward spiral continued…

Housed with fellow lonely, wounded souls heightened my experience of emptiness and desolation. I spent my days searching for a new way to exist. I was still breathing, after all. For what purpose, though, I had no clue.

Until I did. And here began my newfound mission in life: *What can I do to destroy myself, and how can I achieve this with excellence?*

I couldn't seem to grab hold of any other purpose apart from self-destruction.

My first friend in the group home was a man named Curt. His gentleness was enticing and the time I spent with him felt peaceful. We often went for walks around the neighbourhood, no real destination in mind.

Then one day he was gone. Hospitalized, apparently.

This disruption in my routine didn't sit well with me. I needed to know why he was gone, and when he would be returning. During our wandering adventures, hopelessness had often cascaded from his lips. I had yet to understand that this could lead someone to try and end their own life.

My friend Curt had decided he was officially done with the world. Done living. And yet his doctor had apparently caught this intentionality before it could manifest.

He was hospitalized for a long time. Long enough that I didn't anticipate ever seeing him again.

The emptiness became that much more prevalent around and within me. Curt's departure led me even further down the rabbit hole of depression and self-harm. During this time, I formulated new destructive ideas.

Soon I was sent off to a mental health treatment centre. The professionals anticipated that group therapy and close monitoring would successfully derail my downward spiral. In reality, I was too hard-bent on destruction. This treatment centre only provided more fuel for the fire.

For the first few weeks, I was allowed access to my vehicle. Since the treatment centre was outside my hometown, I made trips to and from on weekends to see my family. On one such journey, the idea to end my life right there on the road sparked in my mind. Wouldn't it be easy, and fun, to simply speed up and drive as fast as I could, then inadvertently lose control and careen off-course in a fatal crash? It was a thrilling yet passive way to end my failed life.

Game on! The highway whizzed by under me as my car travelled one hundred seventy kilometres per hour.

But I never lost control.

Was I meant to be a race car driver? Was I just too cowardly to jerk the wheel myself? Whichever the answer, I arrived back "home," psychiatric team waiting to greet me. That day I handed them my keys for the last time. A meeting with my doctor soon revealed my dangerous endeavour, and my license was medically suspended.

Too often now, the four walls that contained me were white and bare, the sterile environment void of much more than germs. It was void of life entirely. I was clothed with a sleek hospital gown and mesh slippers. Having a window to the outside world was a luxury.

But what worth was it at this point to have a vision of blue skies and trees blowing in the wind? The outside world was an anomaly of existence. I felt no connection to it, because I no longer felt hope of any kind. I no longer recognized God in my days. He was the distant memory of a girl who no longer had residence in my heart or mind.

The only real irritation of the walls that held me captive was the lack of easy access to the tools I needed to strive towards self-destruction. Engaging my inner creativity, I scanned the vacuous décor of hospital wards and rated everything I saw on a scale from potentially harmful and attainable, to neither/nor. The higher the rating, the more time I spent thinking about it.

I was successful, to a degree. If nothing else, I kept the nurses on their toes with my frequent disastrous attempts. This added meaning to the emptiness of my days.

In the early years of institutional living, in a moment of frustration, my studious psychiatrist walked me over to another young girl lying in a bed, absent and alone. Scars from self-harm lined her arms like train tracks, extending the full length from wrist to elbow.

Rationally, the doctor posed this question: "Do you want to end up like this girl?"

I bowed my head. "No."

Inwardly, though, I studied these train tracks and declared to myself that I would do a better job than what this damaged soul had done. *Her* scars were decent, but *mine* would be stellar.

Over the course of the next few years, I changed my methods for inflicting wounds, opting for boxcutters which made far deeper cuts far faster. Looking down at my arms, I could see the progress. I was going to reach my goal—and the deeper the wounds, the better they shone in my mind.

When a wound warranted a trip to ER, that was a job well done. And when I ran out of space on my forearms, meaning I had to open a wound over older scars, this was a badge of honour.

I was no longer satisfied by simple scars. I needed them to be uglier. And I found this in burn wounds. The intense experience I discovered—sizzling and popping flesh as I bore down fiery heat on my skin—was startlingly soothing. I'd inhale deeply, pressing down a ferocious curling iron, holding it firmly, extensively. When it came to burn wounds, I measured my success in terms of how long and how hard I could press and hold down the iron—the deeper and longer, the better.

An oddly familiar scent accompanied these grotesque occasions, like bread starting to burn in a toaster. It added yet another twisted knot to the already destroyed ball of yarn that was my life.

Burn wounds were no laughing matter to the professionals who cared for me. I required constant care from nurses to medicate and dress the wounds. Sometimes they took months to heal. Often the healing process was interrupted by my disturbing fascination with pulling back the scabs and reopening the wounds. This created a level of pain even more intense than the original hurt.

The wounds were deep. Two times, for five large burn wounds in total, I required skin grafts. My left thigh still bears the memory of flesh peeled off to cover the open, raw expanse of defunct skin across my arms.

As I look down at my scars on the other side of this story, they are extravagantly large and consuming. *Stellar* might be the word for it, if I were still living in that hopeless space. But I can no longer use that term. It sounds too fantastic and silly a word for a healthy mind to attribute to such a display of brokenness.

My psychiatrist treated me with electroconvulsive therapy (a.k.a. shock therapy), zapping my brain for nine sessions to effectively rid me of my wayward thinking. But I only longed all the more to be slain by this barbaric remedy. My discussions with him sent his head spinning from all the symptoms I displayed. I was only nineteen years old, yet so confused and so profoundly distressed.

My doctor was at a loss as to how to treat me. I was sent to a new hospital in a new city, and I hated it. It was the Siberia of bitterly cold, deadly places. At one point in my stay, I shared a room with a young woman so disturbed that she would intentionally spread her faeces all over the bathroom. All over. Disgusting.

Yet I stayed and appeased the staff by answering many questionnaires and assessments, given in an attempt to figure me out and come up with an appropriate diagnosis. If there was a box I fit into, they would find it and assign it. Or so they thought.

This locked-down wasteland could only hold me captive for so long before I determined to escape, and one day I made a run for it. The downfall of my mission: I hadn't prepared well enough. I had only the clothes on my back. No food. No money. I wouldn't get very far.

But that day, that freedom-day, I walked the streets for as long as my feet would carry me. I had no idea where I was and no idea where I wanted to get to—liberation from my Siberian prison was all I was able to process.

Along my expedition, I hiked across overpasses that posed the question, "Wanna jump from my heights?" I sat and indulged each query. On one bridge, I leaned over and watched the traffic rushing past below. From the depths of my broken heart, I wondered if I could indeed make this moment count, if I could indeed make it the end.

Suddenly, I was startled from my daze by a woman's voice yelling out from her car, "Jump, why don't ya!"

I kept walking.

Looking down, my shoelaces called up to me, "Unfasten us so we can help you. See that fence over there? We can make something work for both of us." Tempting indeed. I sat and untied them. Then I retied them onto the fence, with the dutiful rhythm of a minimum wage worker at a sweat shop. But were they true to their promise? No. I couldn't make our plan come into fruition.

I kept walking. Police cars toured the neighbourhood and I hid from them in fear. Were they searching for me? By now, fatigue and a parched throat weakened my resolve. When my eyes met the scenery in front of me, I recognized my surroundings and determined to walk back into the wasteland from which I had escaped.

Each painful step up towards the unit stomped the bitterness of yet another defeat into my spirit. Terror consumed me as I edged closer and closer towards the locked unit I so despised. The voices of those who would greet me were almost too much to bear.

Yet I continued. Too broken. Too empty. Too thirsty. I had nothing left, and nowhere else to go. I would endure the criticism and scorn, just to meet with the relief of the bed that awaited me and the numbing medication that would soon follow.

A GOOD ENOUGH STORY

Swollen, tender wounds
Defaced her hands
As trespassed graffiti on quality architecture

The Princess dumped her basket's treasures
With a sigh and angry cry
She punted the basket
And watched it fly through the air.

Catapulted by defeat
Its landing sparked epic sprays
Of wicker into the atmosphere

The basket was now broken and limp
Cast aside in the beauty of its habitation.

Satisfaction broke her tear-stained visage
Then her foot pivoted
Purposed and passioned

And the Princess walked off into the distance
Pained
Broken
Angry
Longing

Six:
More Bitter Brokenness

I spent many Christmases in care facilities of various forms. "Jingle Bells" and "We Wish You a Merry Christmas" just don't sound the same in the echoing halls of mental health homes or hospital wards. Christmas lights just don't glow the same off the medical walls meant to keep you alive and safe. There's certainly no joy in opening a random gift of travel-size lotions on Christmas morning.

It was a lonely time. No one understood me, and no one seemed to make sense of my chaotic endeavours to destroy myself. Professionals offered varied responses to my treatment; indifference, laughter, or down-right annoyance were commonplace. This either pushed me to try harder and do better next time, or left me in a place of deeper defeat and self-loathing. At least their odd expressions of compassion offered my weary heart some momentary relief. Love still existed, yet I was unsure of how or why.

Beyond the herd of professionals surrounding me, my only other social connections were with equally broken souls. This was my world, and within it I was a standout kind of character, the kind no one else there had either seen or been—outwardly a gentle teddy bear fit to be squeezed and inwardly a raging grizzly on a relentless attack.

My self-harm didn't end with flesh wounds. I also attacked my internal organs with countless drug overdoses.

If they kill me, great, I thought. *If not, at least they'll harm my kidneys and liver along the way.*

Medications intrigued me, not only because of my previous love of biology and the human body but because of my ability to understand the harm that specific side effects could create.

How dark. How exciting. Hopelessness is like a man thrown overboard, treading water till his legs are numb and he sees no rescue in sight. My legs had been numb for too long, and my rescuer had abandoned me.

My anger prevented me from reaching deep inside and clinging to the biblical promises I had breathed of deeply in my youth. Ending the torturous labour that was my existence seemed like a welcome, and eternal, rest.

While an overdose was taking my last breath one day, I suddenly became afraid. Panicking, I called 911 without knowing why. Maybe it was God at work? Whatever the case, the paramedics arrived. Good thing I had unlocked the door for them, since I was already losing consciousness as they entered my apartment that day. Their words were quick and their hands steady. I gagged as the cold, clawing laryngoscope extended down my throat… and then there was nothingness.

When I awoke, the blank walls and beeping monitors of an ICU room greeted me. The tube in my throat provided my mind with a startling reset. Death had almost won. I cried, my tears stinging and my throat burning. The bitterness of that moment was beyond compare.

Glancing down at my feet, I noticed a ballooned blister—the size of a tennis ball—jiggling across the top of my right foot. I had no recollection of inflicting wound. Where had it come from?

It was quite some time before the endotracheal tube was removed—and longer still before my throat felt healed enough for me to speak my concern to the nurse.

"Sorry about that, hun," she explained. "We were in a hurry to start an IV on you and your arms are so damaged that we needed to put it in your foot. But the first attempt there was unsuccessful and the fluid went interstitial. That blister is quite nasty looking! But it will go away soon enough."

"Oh," was all I could croak out in reply.

My fascination with this blister entertained me until exhaustion again kicked in and I fell into a deep, medicated sleep.

Rather than returning home right after my ICU stay, the doctor transferred me to my posh estate in the psychiatric ward. No welcome-home banners, no cake—just another round of wasted days and medication to effectively numb my existence. I had a daily rotation of four medication dispensing times, averaging six pills each. That's not to mention the as-needed doses administered in between, when I simply couldn't wait for the next round of relief.

Like a teething baby unable to contain the excessive drool building in their mouths, my shirts were regularly soaked with saliva. I was helpless against the free-falling drool. Attractive, coming from a woman in her twenties? I think not.

My head felt as heavy as a bowling ball atop my neck, and so it hung sloppily over to the right. My neck was too weak to hold it upright. Try though I might, it continued to fall back over into its new niche. I looked like a slobbery, sleepy, half-dazed mess of a human. A sad sight to witness for those who'd known me before all this, but it was simply my new, detestable norm.

My desperate, poignant quest to destroy my body had been an ineffectual mess. My attempts to finalize my failures were themselves weirdly humorous. I was now a full-blown disaster, both outwardly and inwardly.

Hopelessly lost. Hopelessly forsaken.

Years into this pained existence, I lived in an apartment complex situated beside a cemetery. On my sunnier days, I rode my bike through it, breathing in the fresh air and releasing my rage into the expanse of headstones. On cloudier days, I peeked outside my window to inhale the rows of solemn emptiness.

My last suicide attempt was to be memorable. I walked into the cemetery with a chef's knife, intent on ending things with a deep slit to my wrist and a stab to my guts. My lifeless body would drape the lifeless ground in a poetic statement of grief.

Standing on the pavement at the edge of the cemetery, I sighed heavily and began with my wrist. The blood pooled onto the cement by my feet, and I felt a rush pass over me.

Next would be the stab wound, but for a moment I second-guessed myself. Was this for real? Was this finally the end?

I drew the knife into my abdomen with surprising ease. Then I slowly released the weapon and simply stared at it, and waited…

I waited for the pool of blood to grow. I waited for my knees to get weak and wobbly.

I waited. Then I cried.

Nothing was happening.

The ultimate brokenness I felt carried me back upstairs into my apartment. I washed my hands and put away my defective weapon. Trudging back down the stairs, I made my way through the fog of night to the ER to have my wounds stitched.

If it were at all possible to compound my despair and defeat that night, the doctor succeeded with his mindless banter: "So what did you use to stab yourself here?"

I described the blade as being approximately four inches long, the entirety of which had entered my body.

"Huh. Well, it would have needed to be far longer if you had hoped to cause *real* or fatal damage."

"Right."

My spirit sank as I took in the deeper reality of his statement: the years of psychiatric medication had created a cesspool of negative side effects, including excessive weight gain. I had become obese. Clearly my judgment had proved inept in factoring in the length of the blade needed to reach my internal organs.

In simply stating the facts, this doctor only enhanced my despair, reminding me that not only was I *crazy*, but also downright *fat*.

Stitches complete, I floundered home. Compounded defeat. Exponential brokenness. Days merged together in a pointless compilation of emptiness.

Were it not for an imminent life-changing encounter, my life would likely have either stagnated or ended permanently in another volatile expression of my hopeless impairment.

Thankfully, oh so thankfully, Jesus soon stepped into my marred existence to free me from the chains that held me, gangrenous and bereft.

Her glazed eyes spanned ahead
Nothing but ugliness here
Parched
Dry ground

Cacti—crowding her pathway
With multiplied thorny soldiers
Bent on further revenge

Tumbleweeds befriended her
Intrigued her
With their wind-inspired wandering
Fulfilling her deep longings
As a bandage
Fulfills a wound's grotesque need to heal

Gloomy clouds loomed overhead
The Princess was tired
The soles of her shoes
Worn
From trudging untended paths so far from home

Seven:
A Grace-Filled Introduction

"Do you see that rabbit over there, staring me down?" my roommate whispered, bug-eyed with fear. "Do you see the gun he's holding, too?"

It had been an ordinary day. We had ridden the bus side by side for the past four hours, just to pass the time. Now, back home and with a tuna casserole split between us, we slouched into the couch and zoned out with a movie.

But our minds were still playing tricks on us.

Becky was a diagnosed treatment-resistant schizophrenic. With matted hair and a smell that could rival a sloth, she was the one person in the world who adored me—needed me even. While a hallucinated evil rabbit harassed Becky's sanity, my own evil angst harassed mine. The companionship between Becky and me was a lifeline in a world that didn't understand us.

It was a normal occurrence for one of us to be spending time in the hospital. While one was an inpatient, the other would come almost daily to visit.

On one of these occasions, Becky was the inpatient and I her visitor. Our mundane, unhealthy lives were about to be disrupted by none other than God Himself.

Bzzzzzzz. I stepped back and waited impatiently for a security guard to let me into the locked psychiatric ward. The door soon swung open and I sauntered inside. I gave the guard half a smile, scrawled my name on the guest sheet, then walked to the nurses' desk.

I carried a heavy load: two six-packs of Diet Coke and a huge dollar store stash of treats to satisfy Becky's frenzied diet: mounds of chocolate, candy, and pepperoni sticks. Though already being treated for early stage diabetes, Becky disregarded her diet recommendations and sought much-needed pleasure from these snacks.

"So, how are you today?" asked the nurse, whom I happened to know and dread. Dutifully she browsed the bags I had brought to ensure the unit's safety standards were met.

"Oh, you know…"

Nodding politely, she passed the bags back over to me.

My insides churned as I swallowed the bitter taste of contempt I had for this woman. Too many times, my brokenness while an inpatient had led to war between us. When we conversed, it was like spewing daggers, sweetened with professional etiquette. We had no common ground. No understanding. She was masterfully composed, confident, and accomplished; I was pathetically flawed, scarred, and insignificant.

Walking away from the desk, I shook off the contemptuous interaction.

"Here ya go!" I said as I walked into Becky's room, tossing the loot onto the crumpled and dirty bed.

Grinning, she began to dig in and gorge herself on the goods.

Then the two of us sat. And sat. Nonsensical conversations sometimes emerged from our frequent idle sittings, but most often we were satisfied to sit in companionable silence.

We heard a knock at the door of Becky's room. No cause for alarm. Professionals were regularly probing and prodding, beginning with a knock, when you were a guest in their suites.

Becky and I looked up, and then we both did a doubletake.

"Ahem, hello," said one of the four people standing in the doorway. "My name is Darren, and this is Daniel, Clayton, and Jaclyn. We care about people and we love God. We believe God has called us to come and pray for people who are sick in the psychiatric ward. We want you to know that God loves you, and He can heal you of your illness. May we come in and chat with you some more?"

Becky looked warily at me, and then waved the group into the room.

The four of them were distinct. Darren was a tall man, football-player-sized, with a bald head and warm smile, his eyes alight with passion. Next was Daniel, smaller in stature and dark-skinned. His eyes held a similar passion and his smile was as genuine as they get. Clayton and Jacyln looked slightly younger. They seemed close in age to me, except well-dressed and exceptional.

Healthy young people, seeking to engage with the likes of Becky and me? This was odd indeed.

The motley missionary crew made themselves as comfortable as the shoebox space would allow. They conversed with Becky and asked questions about her illness. What were her symptoms? For how long had she been struggling? Their words were like a sponge to her parched soul. She soaked up the attention and love and clung to their every word.

When Darren asked if he could pray for her, she nodded excitedly—not because she necessarily believed this was going to heal her, but because these people loved her just as she was.

During this holy meeting, I sat chameleon-like in my chair. I glared at the visitors, my eyes full of black ugliness, as though to hiss, *Don't you dare come near me*. I knew their kind, I knew their God. Or so I thought. I wanted nothing to do with them or Him.

"And what is your name?" Darren asked, turning his attention to me.

With a sigh, I gave away my identity and then looked out the window intently.

"Can we pray for you, too?"

"Absolutely not."

With a sincere smile, he said, "Okay. Well, it was nice to meet you girls today. If you don't mind, Becky, we'll come back to pray with you tomorrow. God loves you."

And then they were gone.

But darn, if they weren't true to their words and returned the next day. And the next.

Becky now waited for her new friends with eager expectation. When they prayed for her, hands on her forehead or forearm, she immediately felt lighter. Her voices left her and her hallucinations disappeared. No medication had yet offered her such relief.

I, on the other hand, continued to rue their too-good-to-be-true, lovey-dovey prayer visits. But I didn't mention these feelings to my friend.

Soon after these encounters, Becky was discharged from the hospital and invited to a Sunday evening Bible study at Darren's home. She begged me to come along for moral support. Knowing she needed help navigating the bus route to find his house, I knew I would have to go whether I wanted to or not. I couldn't abandon my inept yet eager roomie.

A GOOD ENOUGH STORY

Still angry
Bitter
Her calloused hands bore permanent reminders of her folly

Trusting the beauty of her home
The love of her Abba
Her intent to bubble with joy all her days
Absent from harm

Such a lie
Bought and packaged with a bow
Then ripped apart with savage haste

She suffered
Daily
Maybe most with loneliness

Somewhere rooted below the fury
Was the longing for Abba's warm embrace
But like a festering gash in her heart
The sick smell of tender memories
Was quickly shaken off

Replaced with resolve
To continue down this new forged path
Of defeat

When, suddenly
The clouds broke

A ray of sunshine darted boldly as a laser
Interrupting her current brood
And illuminating a shadowed cove up ahead.

Eight: The Encounter with Mercy

Darren's home was easy enough to find, and also easy enough to comfortably escape into. The living room nook was a cozy circle of couches and chairs with a beautiful picture window on one side. It had an innately peaceful atmosphere that beckoned weary travellers to come, sit, and find rest. Becky was at home instantly.

I sunk into a spot beside her and prepared my mind for the fight ahead. I knew Bible studies, and I wasn't going to have any of this one.

I held strong most of the evening, effectively tuning out the conversation. To this day I couldn't tell you what was spoken. I inhaled the family photos hanging on the walls. I noticed the stairs and the kitchen, and imagined living in a home such as this. There was something significant in the atmosphere that I couldn't put my finger on, but it engaged me, even while I disengaged from the community surrounding me.

Late into the evening, people were ushered into a "prayer chair" to have hands laid on them and receive healing words. Ordinary in nature, the chair was just another seat in which a weary soul could come and find rest. It wasn't assigned its lofty title until it slid over from its nook into the middle of the room.

Everyone eventually sat in the chair that evening, but not me. Not yet.

It was getting very late, and normally I would have long ago passed out in my bed. But here I was in a room of people still full of life and energy. Puzzling.

Was I growing tired? Was my resolve fading? It's hard to say.

An awkward tug of peer pressure called me out as the only one who hadn't yet sat in the prayer chair that night. Would I go, too? Somehow, my feet dragged me up and over to its dreaded frame. No part of me wanted to be sitting in this chair, yet here I was. My back held me arched up into a rare perfect posture. My hands clenched the edges, as if to keep me from falling into the chaos that threatened to capsize me.

Four hands suddenly landed on my body with a gentle intensity that took my breath away. Prayers started flowing. The first two or so slipped right by, not yet penetrating my caged-up heart.

And then it happened.

Like out of a movie, Jesus's voice suddenly entered the room. He tenderly unlocked the door to my heart and beckoned me softly with His still small voice.

"Oh, precious one. I'm so sorry for the pain you've been walking through. I love you with an everlasting love. Won't you let Me back in? I will heal you and redeem your story and bring forth dreams you've long since thought were dead and gone. You are My treasure. Come. Be. I love you."

Tears fell, hard and ugly. One box of tissue wasn't going to suffice for the simultaneous mixture leaking from my eyes and nose in that moment. I was shaking and couldn't restrain myself.

The prayers continued, and the hands upon me were as of an angelic army, carrying my wounded spirit out of the war zone and into the safety of the Father's pearly castle.

Midnight struck before I made it home that night. Becky had been dozing on the couch at Darren's house that evening, despite the miracle taking place in front of her. Sleep was still a long way off for me. I had a lot to process. Years of grief had just been wiped clean in an unanticipated act of grace. How? Why? Questions needed investigating, emotions needed settling.

Finally, I was met with an exhaustion more exciting than cumbersome. I was alive.

In the months ahead, I immersed myself in worship. I fell in love with artists like Kim Walker and Misty Edwards. They sang with new and exciting passion. I cried. Wept. Tears of relief and tears of joy.

Even the old songs, like "Amazing Grace," were deeply touching; I too had been lost and was now found. I had been blind and now I could see. I really had been a wretch, for ten long years. But I had been loved, even then. Not forgotten. Sought after relentlessly. Kept from death, despite my persistent attempts in my ill and lost state.

I basked in God's love for me, soaked in worship music that led me deeper into God's heart for me. I had never known this type of love. It might seem like an odd statement since I had grown up in a church, piously reading and applying Scripture, but only now did the Gospel message finally reach my heart. I had needed to be broken first, destitute and destroyed, but I now understood.

I craved Jesus more than anything. Streamed sermons and music became my bread and butter, my sustenance for the new life I'd been carried into.

In my youth I had intellectually defined the word *grace*, but it had never made it to my heart. Now I searched to understand it completely. I needed to know that my years of pain had a purpose.

One of the definitions of *grace*, according to Webster, is "the divine favor toward man; the mercy of God, as distinguished from His justice; also, any benefits His mercy imparts; divine love or pardon; a state of acceptance with God; enjoyment of the divine favor."[3] This definition inspired me. It spoke to the impactful moment when Jesus had met me at that Bible study, and I had continued to witness it as I walked forward with newfound freedom.

To be alive is a gift. To be alive with the heart-knowledge of God's love and grace towards us? That is the ultimate gift!

---

[3] *Webster Dictionary*, "Grace." Date of access: July 9, 2020 (http://www.webster-dictionary.net/definition/grace).

This miraculous freedom was not without further struggles. It would be lovely to say everything went smoothly and easily from this point forward, but the reality is that we still live in a world full of sin and hardship and pain. My own internal struggles had taken years to fully develop, so it made sense that diligent, persistent effort would be required to nullify their long-term effects. Ultimately, I know my scars and harmful internal processes won't be fully redeemed until Jesus calls me home.

I still trembled under the flaming arrows of my oppressor. Often, too often, the arrows hit. My mind lost sight of my victorious knight, Jesus, who had come to my rescue and carried me out of the mire.

As time went on, I became too easily lost again in fogs of anguish and pain. The instinct to self-harm screamed from within, needing to be released. To my new faith friends and counsel, I described these moments as an inner spirit screaming, wailing, shrieking to get out. My mind became overwhelmed with visions and sensations of my arms being torn open in the release of this filth.

It was a terrifying time. Would I ever really be free?

Darren held up the shield of faith for me when I was too weak to wield my own. He wisely counselled me, time and again, "You have to close that door, Sara. You will not find freedom until you close it."[4]

He was one hundred percent right, though his patient words fell on deaf ears for a while.

One day, they suddenly connected. My mind was bubbling over with frightful agitation again. Peace was nowhere to be seen, except for in the heat of the stove element nonchalantly stationed a few feet away. I rose from my couch and strode over to it. I rolled up my sleeve, deciding that the edge of my wrist and part of my palm would pay the price today. I hardly had any other healthy flesh left to choose from.

Turning the element's dial to high, I waited for the welcome red hue to flare.

And then I hesitated.

---

[4] By this, he meant that as long as I left the door to self-harm open, it would be an option for me in moments of angst. If it was no longer an option, if I closed the door, I could be free to make other, better, healthier choices.

Not one to dally, today's sudden pause felt different. I stared absently at the element and at my hand. Then I turned the element off and left the kitchen.

What had just happened?

Upon later reflection with Darren, I realized that I had *closed the door*. In the heat of the moment, I had done it subconsciously. And therein lay my victory. I was free.

Moments of boiling-over emotion returned every so often, still with a torturous slew of sensations, but self-harm was no longer an option. I now fought with power. Prayer, worship, and declaring Scripture were my weapons of victory.

On other frustratingly familiar days I'd languish on the couch, the cushion soaking up my tears with steadfast affection. The brokenness in those moments still felt so overwhelming.

Too weak to get up, too distressed and burdened, I sputtered a silent, simple prayer and bravely determined to press on—yet acknowledging I couldn't do it on my own strength.

Reaching for my phone, I turned on my worship playlist and then closed my eyes and listened. Sometimes I croaked out the lyrics.

The sooner I forced the songs out through my own lips, the sooner freedom found me. Sometimes, though, I'd just lay still and silent.

Without the crashing of fireworks, a celebration was taking place. Though I couldn't see it, heaven's angels were dancing and shouting praises of their own. My victory dance was on its way.

It didn't take long. My spirit began to feel lighter. The stain of tears dried along my cheeks. Breathing was no longer a chore. Hope returned.

Stretching, I rose from my ailing recumbency, refreshed. My inner being, winged as an eagle, was free again to soar on the heights.

And soar I did, crashing through barriers that should have kept me stagnant. My story was meeting with victory upon victory, despite the wobbly interludes.

Seduced by the startling display
The Princess sashayed ahead

Standing tall
Draped as a canvas, by flowering vines
Was a carved-out nook of rock

She peeked inside

Dark
Dank
But so enticing

Her hands traced along the inner surface of rock
Step by step
She deepened her trek into the unknown

She thought she heard laughter
Like that of a child
A joy-filled squeal
Whose merriment puzzled her all the more

And then she saw her
A doll of a girl
Chasing after a breathtaking buffet
Of butterflies

Gracefully frolicking
Through sunshine-y fields of daisies

Nine:
The Bumpy, Redeemed Road

I was *on my way, w*itnessing the wonders of a God who, true to His Word, was redeeming my story beyond anything I'd dreamt. Even with the hiccups, I was alive. Free. Ever-learning. Still becoming. Enough.

On a particularly heavy day, I felt thankful for my appointment with Bill, my long-time therapist. He was a wise and gentle man. Deep inside, I secretly longed for him to be my father. His presence was so peaceful, and sitting across from him in that office I felt cared for beyond the chaos exuding from within.

Even before I'd been met by Darren, and later Jesus, Bill had planted seeds of faith in my heart, reminding me of my long-lost relationship with Jesus and my still very real need for God. Though I'd brushed off Bill's words for months, maybe more, I now clung to the hope found within them.

My one-hour sessions with him were a lifeline these days. He knew how to minister to my internal pain with such compassion, freeing me to embrace wisdom and hope. This allowed space between all my self-defeating thoughts for a healthier mindset to grow.

"What exactly is *normal*, anyway?" Bill asked with a grin.

"You know, average. Good productive people. The ones with perfectly cropped hair and naturally composed faces. The ones driving their cars to and from work and going out for drinks with friends on weekends. They are normal."

I was stuck again. I hated that word, always had. *Normal.* It was tied so tightly to my conceptual nemesis, *good enough*, and it always felt out of reach.

My battle with this unforgiving word had flipflopped through the years. Prior to falling off the deep end into hopelessness, *normal* had meant average, and I'd needed to go beyond that into exceptional.

In the middle of my despair and darkness, however, *normal* had shifted to mean genuinely acceptable. My broken heart had despised this definition and despised itself for so completely and eternally missing the mark.

Now, on the redeemed road, *normal* still pestered me. I'd gotten caught in the trap of desperately needing to get back to normal. It was a new marker of *good enough*, but I was still far from attaining it.

My heightened feelings of fatigue and stress told me I still wasn't *normal*. When I started working again, after not engaging with the working world for a decade, fatigue and stress became a regular occurrence. What should have felt like normal was instead a stinging sign that I had missed the mark.

I was a frequent crier, and when the tears started falling they were hard to stop. Many trips out in public were spent with red eyes and a gushy face, despite my deepfelt desire to come across as put-together. It's hard work trying to train a mind that's charted unhealthy pathways for far too long, but these moments were yet another highlight of how far I still was from being *normal.*

My visible scars were a marker that I still wasn't *normal*, like a flashing light on display. For so long my scars had been my passionate pursuit, my glory. Now they induced feelings of shame and disgust. They drew a big ugly circle around my existence, as though to say, "Now here's a messed-up young woman. Steer clear!"

Ugh. How was I to walk victoriously, normally, looking like *this*?

Long sleeves became my trademark style, a coping mechanism to eliminate the sting of shame. But long sleeves are plain uncomfortable in summer, and for some unknown reason my metabolism caused me to heat up way faster than the average person—leaving me sickeningly hot even when others were cold. Not fair in the least, for someone trying to hide their ugliness.

But maybe this was the push I needed to learn to let go of shame and show off my scars with confidence...

Many well-meaning and curious bystanders have asked, "What happened to your arms? Were you in a fire?" Their wide-eyed gazes all too often dart away in communication, but how could they not? Humans are attracted to notable differences in others. The qualities that stand out help us define how we relate to each other.

When at last I understood how profoundly sinister was this nemesis, shame, and how profoundly more awesome was my God, I chose to pray. Sobbing at the feet of Jesus, I lay down my battle with shame. I hated that I'd come so far and yet was still so broken, so defined by my past brokenness.

I determined that I had to be prepared for stares, prepared for questions. This would be my victory strategy. More so, I had to choose to believe my visible signs of brokenness could be a light leading others to hope and stop hiding behind long sleeves.

Let the flags of caution wave. Let the stares and questions come. God was bigger than my brokenness. I had been rescued, and now restored. Even if I had to tell myself this a million times, I would. Because there is no victory if we need to hide in fear.

Bam! Another door slammed shut.

Job interviews, interacting with customers... these were still sometimes terrifying opportunities to openly show my scars. I gave myself pep talks to help me deal with conversations or simple stares.

For job interviews, I rehearsed my confident explanations for the scars, emphasising their place in the past rather than the present. For customers, I developed concise answers to their inevitable questions.

"Was I in a fire? Oh." I'd pause to examine my arms. "No. No fire. I wish! No, I'm kidding..."

Looking into their questioning eyes, I would determine if the timing was right. This light and witty response was sometimes all a person needed, or wanted, to hear—it set their minds at ease enough to continue on with their day.

But there were those who needed to hear more. Their *hearts* needed it. There was brokenness in their story, too. Maybe not in the same stamped ugliness, but it was there and it cried out for relief. And so, I'd engage deeper.

"For many years I struggled with depression and hopelessness," I would say. "These are self-inflicted wounds. I'm just grateful they represent my past. I'm not the same person anymore."

With a deep breath, I'd release the anxiety that came with vocalizing these words.

I was blessed when people replied, "Well, isn't that wonderful to hear." They'd smile and we'd part ways. A tiny seed of faithfulness had been planted, and the Lord would take it from there.

Despite the moments I still battle with *normal* and the many triggers that would love to send me spiralling in defeat, my faith is now secure. I won't go down into deep despair again. My eyes have seen the glory and goodness of God at work redeeming my life. He continues to show up and prove to me His faithfulness. This hope is my victory.

After ten long years of emptiness, God has led me from glory into glory, as promised.

Back in the day, had a doctor asked me if I ever saw myself working or getting married or thriving in motherhood, I would have simply laughed. Perhaps he would have been crazy himself. These opportunities I've since had are nothing short of miraculous gifts by the grace of an all-powerful, all-knowing God who loves me. How can I not choose hope now, even on the hard days?

A GOOD ENOUGH STORY

Who was this doll,
This darling delight?

Her hair bounced with each light-hearted step
Her dress twirled with each leisurely lunge
Her smile
Pure innocence

The Princess needed to know
And so she stepped forward to engage

Tapping the girl's shoulder
To awaken her from merry oblivion
She swivelled and swooned
The epitome of grace
Then reached out to the Princess
For a warm embrace

Backward steps
This offering felt too much
Too raw
Too awkward from her long
Stagnant solitude

And yet she yearned
To feel such welcome
Secure
Love

Ten:
God-Breathed Embraces, Forged from the Ashes

Along the healing road of redemption in my story, I've been given another gift from God—to see a person's spirit from looking into their eyes. I'm reminded of the following scripture:

> *Blessed be the God and Father of our Lord Jesus Christ, the Father of mercies and God of all comfort, who comforts us in all our tribulation, that we may be able to comfort those who are in any trouble, with the comfort with which we ourselves are comforted by God.* (2 Corinthians 1:3–4, NKJV)

Out of my own brokenness, I now saw brokenness in others. And it came from looking into their eyes. A French proverb says, "The eyes are the mirror of the soul." A popular variant of this tells us, "The eyes are the window of the soul."[5]

I've seen sadness in others' eyes that goes deeper than tears could ever expose—often when engaging in surface-level, informal conversation. Hidden heartache lurks in so many seemingly normal, happy people—it's latent yet longs to be realized and released. I've

---

[5] Gregory Y. Titelman, *Dictionary of Popular Proverbs and Sayings* (New York, NY: Random House, 1996).

seen eyes that hold bitter darkness, pointing to a deep void. They remind me of the void in my own spirit for so many years, and I assume that my own eyes looked similarly that first day I met Darren, Daniel, Clayton, and Jaclyn.

Like bait fish in shark-infested waters, this world is full of hurting hearts. People are terrorized by fear, defeated and wounded. My heart breaks for them.

I began to engage my God-given gift to see the brokenness in others, all the while aching to be a vessel of hope in their stories—scars and all. I knew the value of an embrace. I knew that the compassionate declaration "You are loved; your story isn't over yet" could mean the difference between life and death for so many. I knew because I had lived it, and because God was opening my eyes, heart, and mind to give me opportunities to comfort others in their own hardships.

In recent years, I've been given many opportunities to initiate conversations with those who are hurting. Seeing the pain in their eyes, I use my scars to point them towards hope.

Valerie was one such person. I was riding the bus, not yet having been given the chance to earn back my driver's license after years of medical suspension, when she happened to approach me in need of a seat.

"Can I sit here?" she asked timidly.

I looked up from my phone, headphones in and worship music playing, and smiled. I nodded, moving my bag onto my lap.

"Thanks."

I removed my headphones and turned off the music. Recognizing this woman from previous bus trips, I decided today would be a good day to begin a conversation. Maybe I'd make a new friend!

"I'm Sara," I said. "What's your name?"

"Valerie."

I grinned. "Nice to meet you, finally!"

Twenty minutes riding side-by-side was enough time to hear some of her story and realize that my own story could impact hers. I found out she had moved to the city after fleeing an abusive relationship, and she was now quite alone. I further learned that she struggled with depression, and, wouldn't you know it, self-harm.

I rolled up my sleeves. It happened to be cooler this day, so I'd chosen long sleeves despite my newfound bravery to no longer hide in shame.

"I struggled with self-harm for many years, too." I said. "It was a really dark, really hard place to live in. But I made it through. There's hope, Valerie."

Her eyes lit up. She spoke no memorable words, but those eyes beheld hope that day. God could use this moment to take her out of her own bitter pain and into freedom.

I didn't make a new friend, per se, but our frequent bus run-ins presented many follow-up smiles and brief conversations. We shared a secret. Her story wasn't hidden, and neither was mine. We were known. Love was known. Hope could be found.

I don't know where Valerie is these days. I pray she's found freedom and victory. I pray she's met with the ultimate lover of her soul and giver of hope, Jesus. Her name, her story, are a part of mine now, all because we shared more than just a seat on a bus one day.

Another opportunity presented itself while I was working at a pharmacy in a busy mall. Stationed at the drop-off desk, I greeted a young girl who had a prescription to be filled. I don't remember her name, but I remember her face and our conversation.

She handed me a prescription for an antidepressant and antianxiety medication.

"Are these medications new for you?" I politely asked.

It was an appropriate question. To more accurately care for our patients, we need to be aware of their medical history.

"Yes," the girl said. "I was on this other medicine before, but it was making me feel sick."

"I see."

I entered the required information into the computer and told her that her medications would be ready in a half-hour.

My hands counted out pills and my voice answered phones, but I was distracted; my heart prayed as my mind prepared to catch her again at the pickup counter. The pain emanating from her eyes had been intense. Piercing. Agonizing. She needed hope.

When I spotted her approaching the pickup counter, I jumped up from my designated area to meet her—perhaps to my boss's annoyance.

"They're ready for you!" I smiled. "Do you have any questions for the pharmacist?"

"No. I'm sure the instructions are straightforward."

I smiled and told her she could always call later if she did have questions. While scanning the barcode, I then leaned over the counter and whispered a few words: "You are a beautiful young girl. Your life has so much potential. We all have our stories…" I pointed down to my arms. "… and this isn't the end of yours."

Then the tears fell. She didn't speak much, but she nodded and walked away.

At first, I felt afraid. Had I made things worse?

Oh no! God, help me! Help her! I prayed for her more, then tried to focus my attention back on my job. The interaction got lost in the haze of my busy work and home life.

A month or two, or six, went by, and then the girl suddenly reappeared at the pharmacy. I recognized her face as I greeted her at the pickup counter, but I didn't immediately remember the intimacy of our previous interaction.

She smiled confidently as she took her prescription.

"I wanted to thank you for talking to me here a while ago," she said. "You have no idea how much your words impacted me. Thank you for caring about me, without knowing me."

Now it was my turn to shed some tears. Our previous conversation flashed back through my memory and my heart sang as I realized my small effort, presented messily, had sparked hope in her.

That's my God. That's my Redeemer, still working to redeem others' stories. I love being a part of the beauty in this.

Am I *normal* yet? I'm still a living, breathing, walking caution sign. And I still sometimes battle the ugliness that comes from my scars, a nagging reminder of where I used to be. Days and weeks can go by without me noticing my scars at all. Then, somewhat suddenly, I'll see them again and be caught off-guard by their vulgar presence.

Oh yeah, that's me, I'll think, sighing as my guts sink with a deep thud. *Yuck.*

Photographs are among the big horror-show reflections for me. While some women zone in on their double chin or too-big nose, it's my scars that jump out at me. Because they were self-inflicted, they threaten my peace. The double chin and too-big nose are beyond a woman's control. She can hopefully let these parts of herself go and see her innate beauty. But what if it's the deeper parts of me that have *caused* my scars? Can I love them? Can I love the one who wielded the blows?

This is a battle I'm learning to fight—or better yet, learning to release. It's not one I'm meant to win. Loving oneself outwardly is hard enough. Loving my inner ugliness takes the battle to a whole other level—to much needed, freely offered *grace*.

It's a profound concept, but I'm learning.

SARA KENNERLEY

The girl reached out for her hand
Ushering the Princess forward

Offer accepted

Princess!
Your hands!
So calloused! So raw!
What a story you must have!

Alas, a hopeless, pitiful one…

Oh, no
Sweet Princess
Your Abba is too awesome
To let despair and depravity win

He's promised to work all things for good
To create beauty from ashes
To bring joy from sorrow

Have you shown Him your hands?
Told Him your hurt?

No no. I couldn't, I won't...
Look at me -
Ragged
An utter disappointment
To such a perfect Abba

Silly Princess
He loves you
Always has, always will

Go Home.

Tears falling once more
Hard
Fast
Healing tears

And this time the Princess
Reached out to the doll-like girl
Now Friend
For the warm embrace her heart craved

Hope
Restored

Eleven:
The Fibromyalgia Roadblock

Continuing on the freedom road, my spirit had a zest to be fully alive, fully present, fully engaged. I had ten years of my life that I needed to catch up on, so much to do and experience. I wanted more beauty, more wonder. I took the following Bible verse to heart, anticipating the abundance in my own life as I yielded my heart anew to Jesus.

> *The thief comes only to steal and kill and destroy. I [Jesus] came that they may have life and have it abundantly.* (John 10:10, ESV)

Even after partaking of glorious victory, the shame of my scars transforming into hope, my battles with *normal* and *good enough* were far from over. About a year into this excited, wonder-filled state of being, my body began to cry out with widespread pain, fatigue, and heaviness. I could barely crawl out of bed. Every part of my body ached, beyond the chronic back pain I'd had since childhood.

What was going on? This didn't feel fair at all.

I was soon diagnosed with fibromyalgia, and its presence has frustrated me in my drive to be all I long to be in this new abundant life.

Prior to this diagnosis, I adamantly believed a key marker of my success lay in my ability to let go of the disability pay I'd been receiving from the government. Since my days of hospitalization, that money had kept me housed and fed. It was still my main source of income, covering my rent and major bills, although I also worked part-time at the pharmacy.

Successful people around me exclaimed that this government aide was a crutch and a cop-out, and their adamance only increased the pressure I placed on myself. I absorbed the lie that my worth and identity were tied to the government's money, and I would never be free and successful until I could work full-time and walk away from government support.

I determined to develop a career and devout my days to full-time work like the rest of the world. Then I'd be a shining star, an example of a masterfully redeemed life. That was the marker I set for myself, and I'd get there.

Then, wham: fibromyalgia. A single eight-hour shift took every ounce of my energy, and then some. I wasn't just *tired*. I was completely spent. My muscles ached, but more so, they whimpered and shook from the effort of keeping me upright.

Fibromyalgia was the ultimate betrayal of my body towards my spirit. I craved life and I wanted everything I could grab hold of.

Now, I could barely get through one day.

Normal? Far from it. And it now looked as though I never really would be.

I discovered another force working against me in my struggle with fibromyalgia: the more exhausted I felt, the more pain I was in, the lower my mood crashed. Recognizing this downward spiral was a huge blow. I hated myself for so easily dipping into a place I'd vowed never to return to. My inner hate only made the mood issues harder to manage.

I've since found solace in humble vulnerability, in choosing to reach out and share my brokenness and struggles. I was insistent that I needed to share my heart with laymen, with friends and non-professionals—not from a place of disregard for the benefit of professionals, but from longing to be seen and welcomed into the world of *normal* I so craved.

Would God hear and understand this cry from deep within? Certainly. He's continued to place willing friends alongside me in my redeemed journey, friends okay with my vulnerable, messy moments and not frightened away by them.

My heart has still been plagued with one big question, though: *Why, God?*

Ultimately, I know the why questions humans wrestle with won't fully be answered until we reach heaven one day. But still I ponder, in a search for peace.

When it comes to healing, there's a huge split in the church's theology. Arguments from both sides have captured my attention and left me stuck somewhere in the middle. On one hand, I absolutely believe God can heal any and every ailment. On the other hand, I know that in this life we will have suffering. Jesus gave His disciples authority to heal the sick and cast out demons, yet Paul himself was left with a thorn in his flesh. He cried out to God for relief from it and was told, "No, God's grace is sufficient for your every need."

These two pieces of the puzzle seem to be at odds with each other—until I resolve them in God's sovereignty. In the midst of the absolute frustration of chronic pain and fatigue, when I feel broken and less than who I want to be, I still adamantly choose to trust God's faithfulness and love for me, and so in that settled place I can move forward in peace.

I've also come to believe that these pain issues remain partly to keep me humble, looking to Jesus for strength. My innate determination to strive on my strength is tethered to this pain and fatigue. It reins me in, back to where I know my heart needs to be: securely tied to God's identity within me and His ability to take me much further than I could ever go on my own.

Some days are still such a struggle, though! Yet these days are when His mercy shines through all the more. Maybe not right away. I first have to push past my own emotions and defeat.

But when I cry out in prayer, when I exit my funk and press in to Him despite the pain, that's when I come alive. That's when my day transforms into something beautiful.

Paul's writing in 1 Corinthians 13—the "love chapter," as it's so eloquently been coined—speaks much life and hope into my struggle with fibromyalgia:

> *When I was a child, I spoke like a child, I thought like a child, I reasoned like a child. When I became a man, I gave up childish ways. For now we see in a mirror dimly, but then face to face. Now I know in part; then I shall know fully, even as I have been fully known.* (1 Corinthians 13:11–12, ESV)

It's interesting to me that these wise words are placed in the "love chapter." In our search to understand how God's perfect love can allow us to walk through pain and hardship, it's important to grasp this truth: God's love never ends, and it will never fail us. Part of growing up means letting go of our toddler-like motivation to ask *why* a hundred million times a day. Becoming more mature means trusting the relationship that has been established between me and God, who has proven faithful time and again, then stepping forward despite my dim perspective.

And so this fibromyalgia roadblock has ushered me deeper in my faith, keeping me humble, though many days I still cry out for relief. I trust the God who holds my hand. I'm leaning on His strength and continuing to walk out the abundant life He's provided for me.

Maybe one day before I reach heaven I'll see healing and relief. Until then, and even if not, I'm learning to be settled in truth. I'm still questioning my arrival at *normal* and *good enough*, but also still holding my heart open for God to use and transform me despite my inadequacies.

Walk home with me, Friend, hold my hand
I'm weak
Wounded
Raw

Dear Princess, these butterflies beckon me to stay
And your Abba has promised
To give you all you need
To make it back home

Walk
Eyes open and looking up
He'll see you coming from afar
And start running toward you
I promise

But, but…

Have faith…

And so
Another healing hug
And a holy kiss

Then the Friend spotted more beautiful butterflies
And pranced off
Pleased and perfectly peaceful

The Princess paused
Looked up with a sigh

Doubting, but hopeful
Weary, but energized
Afraid, but desperate

For the strength
The love

Found in the shelter of Abba's Kingdom

Twelve:
The Farse of Perfection in Motherhood

Motherhood has been the most wonderful gift I've been given in this redeemed life, and also the most challenging. Whereas I thought I was improving and doing well with letting the Lord lead and release me from my striving tendencies, becoming a mother suddenly heightened the struggle for me all over again. Not that wanting the best for my children is a bad thing!

As a mother, I want to exceed all the prerequisites to ensure my children are healthy. Am I relying more on interactive play and less on screens to entertain them? Are they enjoying the outdoors enough? Are they eating the right foods, and having enough of them? Are they sailing through milestones appropriately?

These questions motivate me even more on a daily basis. Am I instilling in them routines that will nurture their spiritual growth? Do they go to bed free from anxiety and knowing they're loved?

The plethora of information available to mothers is vast and potentially paralyzing. While tackling one seemingly important issue for our children's development, it can feel like fifty more are being ignored. Is perfect parenting even possible? If so, what standards should we aim for?

These questions are a signal that my heart needs to align with the truth. Yet they plague me, even in the knowledge of grace and the redemption and hope I've found in Jesus. In this important role of motherhood I've stepped into, we needn't qualify ourselves with words like "perfect" or "successful."

As one bought and redeemed by grace, motherhood has taught me a new rhythm of daily surrender in the midst of my struggle to do my best. Ever single day. I fight the need to control every conversation, every meal, and every activity.

I suit up in my Wonder Mom cape and aim to fly solo, achieving the goals I've set for myself in terms of raising my children to perfection. But then I crash into the walls of fatigue and incomprehension. Sleep is a necessity and tiny humans are complex creatures. This sends me sputtering, bruised and weary, back to the feet of Jesus. Daily.

How do I reconcile my drive to excel in motherhood with my overwhelming need for grace and surrender? I've yet to conquer this in practice, though I'm growing in wisdom to recognize and seek after the truth. For that I am grateful.

With my firstborn son, I struggled with many first-time mom woes: feeling anxiety at every new milestone and making the crushing transition into the new norm of sleepless nights and foggy days. Yet he and I bonded so closely and I loved him more than life itself. I loved being his mom and felt like I was doing a great job at it, giving one hundred ten percent effort.

When I found out my daughter was coming, and that she was not a he, I was apprehensive and a bit annoyed at God. I had been doing great raising my little boy so far, so why would He give me a girl? The potential for messing up with her was huge, especially since I still felt such angst from my own childhood. Girls scared me. Yet she was on her way. Did God really know what He was doing?

The fear was real.

And then I met her. She charmed with her smile. She delighted her brother, her dad, and me.

I was shocked, to say the least, as my daughter grew. How could it be that she so quickly developed a different personality to her brother? I'd heard people say that no two kids are the same, but I was astonished to watch it happen.

So far in raising my dear children, young as they are, I've noticed two main struggles.

Number one, my son is a sensitive little boy, so sensitive that I worry for him. On my bad days, when I'm tired and consumed by "grouchies," his tender little heart picks up on my mood and he's quick to cry. It annoys me in the moment. I can't even express my own inner struggles and frustrations without worrying about his state of mind. I want to lash out and scream all the more at my inability to be the peaceful, stable influence my kids can always run to.

My Wonder Mom cape is quite lacking in its peace capacity, despite my inner drive to be that for my kids one hundred percent of the time. This begs the question: is eighty-eight percent of the time okay? What about sixty percent? Yikes. I literally shuttered as I typed that number. Any lower and I may have fallen over on the floor.

Number two, my daughter has a spitfire personality. She's determined and vocal about things not going as she'd like. I'm quick to fire back my frustrations, as her ear-piercing screeches rattle me to the core. Her flailing body ignites a fear-filled response in me, so I yell, which I hate. I sometimes throw my own version of a toddler tantrum.

Then my heart breaks as I realize that once again my Wonder Mom's cape has failed. It lacks the perfect patience I've set as the standard.

Many nights I've cried out in prayer while rocking my precious ones to sleep.

My prayer with my son sounds something like this: *Lord Jesus, don't let me hinder this little boy as I raise him. He's so sensitive, which I know You will use in mighty ways. But help me not to bruise his tender heart in the process of growing. This thought really scares me, Lord.*

With my daughter, it sounds like this: *Lord, help me be a better momma to her. Why am I failing so miserably already? I don't want to yell, but I'm so quickly irritated. Give me a more compassionate heart, to see deeper into why she's so fiercely vocal so I can meet her needs for comfort and safety in her own chaos.*

My prayers aren't falling on deaf ears—not these prayers of mine, and not any other prayer sent out from the hearts of longing, desperate souls who know their need for their Creator and Redeemer.

So why do I still struggle with perfection?

I want more. I want to be more. At the surface, I would say that it's so my kids will grow up healthy on all fronts. But deeper? It's because their success would be a marker of my own.

Ouch.

That's a painful thought to express. It has the capacity to send me in two directions: to defeat, because I've selfishly missed the mark of grace once more, or to surrender at the foot of the Cross, where I'll find mercy and healing.

Because of the hope of God's miraculous work all around and in me, I choose mercy. As I sit in mercy, drinking of the life-giving properties it holds, I begin to see a deeper application.

Mercy and forgiveness are key lessons I can teach my children throughout our days. Mistake after mistake, I know that by showing my imperfections to my children—requesting forgiveness and living out repentance—they will ultimately see Jesus. My efforts to raise them well, building a foundation of faith in their own hearts despite my mess-ups along the way, will indeed hold strong in the end, just as Proverbs 22:6 wisely reminds us.

And I'll have been successful in motherhood, despite myself.

A GOOD ENOUGH STORY

The road home to Abba's Kingdom
Glittered
With similar butterfly specimens
That had fluttered around her Friend

A precious reminder
Of the goodness to come

She looked up
Smiling into the sunshine

Then looked down
Still now so cautious of her steps

Once
Twice
Three times, even

Sneaky twigs
Slippery mud
Sharp stones
Set to tumble her

Yet she remained
Upright
Determined

And then, she spotted Him
Running from afar
Just as her Friend had promised

He shone
Brighter than the sun

He stood
Taller than the mountains

He knelt
Then He embraced her

More securely
More fully
More warmly

And the Princess felt settled
More than she'd ever felt before

Thirteen: Hope for the Not-Quites

Reaching the breaking point looks different for everyone. Though our stories carry common threads, they knot up quite uniquely. My breaking point, and my ten-year stretch of walking through a wasteland, was treacherous, to say the least. Your story and your breaking point may be equally treacherous and painful, despite being different.

We are all human. Our hearts bleed the same hurts. We cry the same tears. The bondage of our emotions leaves us similarly broken, lifeless, and in need of hope.

My battle with *good enough* indeed nearly cost me my life. And it still doesn't always sit well, this idea of being not quite good enough. I'm reminded time and again of Paul's words:

> *So I find this law at work: Although I want to do good, evil is right there with me. For in my inner being I delight in God's law; but I see another law at work in me, waging war against the law of my mind and making me a prisoner of the law of sin at work within me. What a wretched man I am! Who will rescue me from this body that is subject to death? Thanks be to God, who delivers me through Jesus Christ our Lord!* (Romans 7:21–25, NIV)

I still want to do everything well. Better than well. Good enough for the standard-setters around me, for God, and also for myself—my ultimate critic. While reflecting on the Scripture's teachings of God's laws, works, and grace, I have a better understanding than I did in my youth. Still, I continue to fight the flesh in me that wants to go at every task placed before me on my own strength, welcoming success with pride-filled open arms.

What a wretched woman I am!

Paul understands... and so does God. He created me, after all, and He knows that I'm living in a sinful world with sinful tendencies.

Here, friends, is our hope, and I will cling to this truth for the rest of my days: Jesus paid the price for my striving. I will never be *good enough*, yet He is and always will be. Even if I have to fall on my knees in tears of despair over another failure, or if I once again fail to avoid the failure trap, there's still hope.

God, through Jesus Christ, will lovingly, faithfully, tenderly, and patiently pick me back up and set my feet back on His sturdy foundation. I will be all right. I am loved. My self-defeating tendencies have no power over the One who defeated death itself.

As much as perfection still chases me, and I it, I believe that I've met with enough failures and grace to know that perfection doesn't define me. My good enough mindset is no match for the God of Creation. The woman He says I am is the ultimate definition of my worth and identity.

On the days I have a hard time remembering and resting in this truth, I stumble. I meet the ground with my knees, wailing and crawling for a while. But when I do look up again, I see mercy smiling down on me. I can rise and wipe away the tears. I can brush off the dust and press on in this blessed life I've been given.

My paternal grandparents were lovers of language. They travelled all over the world and were fluent in seven languages. That is seriously impressive to me. In a limited expression of their excellence, I'm also passionate about languages and enjoyed studying Spanish and German during my school years.

This was partly my reason for considering speech and language pathology as a career choice after graduating high school. I get excited thinking about the root of a word and where it came from. Languages are complex, yet interestingly similar in nature. Pulling from their similarities, I enjoy comparing words and phrases, and would love to have more time to devote to delving into other languages at some point.

Though I likely won't have the opportunity to travel the world and aspire to fluency in multiple languages, I'm appreciative of the love of language my grandparents gave me. Whether this comes across in writing or studying or teaching my children, linguistics is a beautiful way to communicate and understand our world.

Living in our technologically advanced times also makes it quite easy to glean from the efforts of those before me who have studied hard and applied their knowledge of language to further understand and grow.

Allow me to share an example.

Stuck on this idea of perfection, I decided to conduct some research into Bible verses that make mention of perfection. And here is where the real fun begins…

In Greek, a few different words were used to convey the idea of perfection.

The Greek word *teleios* is the main word translated in the New Testament for perfect. Here are the meanings of this word in the original language: "'having reached the end,' 'term,' 'limit,' hence, 'complete,' 'full,' 'perfect.'"[6]

I actually first gained this understanding from my therapist, Bill. He often reminded me that the whole idea of perfection is just a journey to becoming more and more complete. In those sessions, I would hear his words and wish with all my might that I could believe them deep down.

But I couldn't.

Today I try to.

Sometimes it reaches my heart, other times not so much. Maybe this, too, is a sign of me working toward the goal of becoming more complete. Maybe it's not actually a bad thing at all?

---

[6] "Perfect; Perfection," *Bible Study Tools*. Date of access: August 5, 2020 (https://www.biblestudytools.com/encyclopedias/isbe/perfect-perfection.html).

When I look at some of the verses translated from the word *teleios*, it becomes more hopeful to apply a different definition from the list of meanings. For example, Jesus says Matthew 19:21, *"If you would be perfect, go, sell what you possess and give to the poor, and you will have treasure in heaven; and come, follow me"* (ESV).

If I insert other definitions of the word perfect, it would read like this: *"If you would be [complete/full], go, sell what you possess and give to the poor, and you will have treasure in heaven; and come, follow me"* (ESV).

Jesus's statement itself is a sign of growth, in my opinion. Jesus tells us that if our desired destination is perfection/completeness/fullness, we should sell our possessions, start collecting treasures in heaven, and follow Him. The word *follow* implies a journey, taking steps forward toward a destination. I like that. My heart needs that.

Other verses that contain the word *teleios* include Philippians 3:15 and Colossians 1:28, only they use the word "mature" instead of perfect.

> *Let those of us who are mature think this way, and if in anything you think otherwise, God will reveal that also to you.* (Philippians 3:15, ESV)

> *Him we proclaim, warning everyone and teaching everyone with all wisdom, that we may present everyone mature in Christ.* (Colossians 1:28, ESV)

What a thought! Maturity is something that comes with growth and learning, and also with seeking God and asking for it (James 1:5).

Other Greek words translated as "perfect" are *teleioo* ("to perfect," "to end," "complete"), *epiteleo* ("to bring through to an end"), *katartizo* ("to make quite ready," "to make complete"), *akribos* ("accurately," "diligently"), *artios* ("fitted," "perfected"), *pleroo* ("to fill," "to make full"), *katartisis* ("thorough adjustment," "fitness"), *katartismos* ("complete adjustment," "perfecting"), and *telesphoreo* ("to bear on to completion or perfection").[7]

---

[7] Ibid.

I think that last Greek word, *telesphoreo*, is my new favourite, which means "bearing on." This reminds me of a struggle, and indeed life is a struggle. The process of laying down a need to achieve immediate perfection is a struggle.

To understand this concept, it's helpful to remember Jesus's speech when He said that we will have struggles in this life. But we shouldn't stay in that place of struggle, or at least not become weary in it. He finished by commanding, *"But take heart! I have overcome the world"* (John 16:33, NIV).

Take heart!

This could also have been written as, "Have courage! Keep going!"

On the Bible Study Tools website, I spotted a quote from W.L. Walker that caused me to pause in awe of its proficient explanation of the internal battle I've been waging almost all my life. How succinctly this quote explains the truth I still fight with to this day! It's a beautiful reminder that God gives each of us wisdom and specific gifts that together minister to the whole body of believers.

> *Perfection is the Christian ideal and aim, but inasmuch as that which God has set before us is infinite—"Ye therefore shall be perfect, as your heavenly Father is perfect" (Matthew 5:48)—absolute perfection must be forever beyond, not only any human, but any finite, being; it is a divine ideal forever shining before us, calling us upward, and making endless progression possible. As noted above, the perfect man, in the Old Testament phrase, was the man whose heart was truly or wholly devoted to God. Christian perfection must also have its seat in such a heart, but it implies the whole conduct and the whole man, conformed thereto as knowledge grows and opportunity arises, or might be found. There may be, of course, a relative perfection, e.g. of the child as a child compared with that of the man. The Christian ought to be continually moving onward toward perfection, looking to Him who is able to "make you perfect in every*

> *good thing (or work) to do his will, working in us that which is well-pleasing in his sight, through Jesus Christ to whom be the glory forever and ever. Amen* (Hebrews 13:21).[8]

I've always been adept at velcroing concepts into my mind and belief system, and I now see the need to apply the same system to my heart. The words of W.L. Walker sound wonderful. Refreshing. True. But it's in living out this concept where it gets hard. My heart needs to remember the words more than my mind.

Where oh where is some heart-Velcro when you need it, right?

I'm reminded of the same concept I was taught by my English teacher and mentor, Miss J., who spoke into my life about the concept of oil rolling water off a duck's back. I might have said, "Now where can I buy some of that duck oil for my heart? I desperately need some of that stuff."

And here is the answer to the duck oil and heart-Velcro question: it's a Kingdom of God commodity, bought by grace and freely handed out by Jesus Christ—not bought in a store. I can't earn it. I can't buy it. Inasmuch as my heart needs it, I know I need Jesus in order to receive it.

In my battle between my internal critic and the truth of God's Word, I'm still a work in progress. I now know and believe that seeking after and finding perfection—and resting in the not-quite moments along the way—is all a journey.

My state of not-quite is actually okay when considered part of the process of growing more complete, of maturing. If I won't be made fully mature or complete until I reach heaven, then it's absolutely okay for me to embrace my not quite status here on earth and cling to Jesus to fully satisfy my good enough longings inside.

---

[8] Ibid., quoting W.L. Walker.

A GOOD ENOUGH STORY

The Princess looked into her Abba's eyes
More tears falling

Then He reached over to her satchel
And pulled out her glass jar

Tipping it slightly
He noted the error in its volume
And patted the Princess
So gently

From His own pocket He pulled
His own glass jar
Even more precious
Etched with the Princess's initials

And she stared
In awe
At the volume of tears within

She didn't understand how
But not a tear had been missed

All safely stored
Known
Cared about

Just as He'd promised so long ago

Fourteen: New Life, New Name!

What's in a name? Despite William Shakespeare's popularized quote from *Romeo and Juliet*,[9] I'd dare to stand out and say that a name can and does often mean a lot.

At the superficial level, our name is a string of letters and syllables that flow together with the intent of sounding pleasing to the ear. Memorable.

Whole books and websites are devoted to searching for baby names, and it's something parents don't take lightly. We know that the name we receive sticks with us all our days—potentially beautifully and potentially harmfully.

A name's esteem is closely tied to those who've borne it before, and how they've impacted our lives. It only takes one bad association with a name to alter the tone of how we perceive others with that same name.

But beyond the appeal of a name is the understanding that our name labels us. And oh how we love labels. Labels inform and direct us in our decision-making. They can be used wisely, but they are arguably also dangerous. As the English idiom tells us, you cannot judge a book by its cover. We understand the motivation and

---

[9] William Shakespeare, *Romeo and Juliet*, Act II, Scene Two.

instinctual draw towards labels, as well as the potential to be misled by them.

In the Bible, names held deep meaning. A name was often rooted in a person's character in an impactful way. I find it intriguing to read the stories where people's names change during or after pivot points in their lives.

I'd like to share a few of my favourite examples of this phenomenon and dig into their names and stories a bit more. These stories point to the beautiful transformation God longs to accomplish in each of us when we cast off our old labels and live out of our God-given identity.

Jacob becomes Israel. Simon becomes Peter. Saul becomes Paul.

Jacob was a twin, born after his brother Esau. His name translates in Hebrew to mean "holder of the heel" or "supplanter."[10]

The Bible says that Jacob came out of the womb grabbing his brother's heel, and once grown, he assailed his brother's birthright and blessing (Genesis 25:28, 31–33, Genesis 27:36). His name fit.

When Jacob later prepared to meet his brother—who'd wanted to kill him since losing his birthright and blessing—he ended up wrestling with God. It was during this defining moment that his name changed. The Lord told him that he was no longer Jacob, but Israel, because he'd wrestled with God and lived (Genesis 32:24–30).

The importance of the new name? Jacob's life had been marked by deception to get what he wanted. When he saw God face to face, when he wrestled with Him and God dealt graciously with him (Genesis 33:10–11), he found favour. His life changed. He had a new name, and therefore a new definition of his character.

Jacob's lineage formed the people of Israel, God's holy, chosen people. These people were those whom God formed covenants with, whom He loved and cherished, and whom He sought to teach and discipline and direct towards Himself and His heart—towards the *real abundant life* found in following after Him.

Next up is Simon, who was a fisherman. The name Simon means listener, or "he has heard."[11] Not a bad name at all. Not a bad

---

[10] "Jacob," *Behind the Name*. Date of Access: August 22, 2020 (https://www.behindthename.com/name/jacob).

[11] "Simon," *Behind the Name*. Date of Access: August 22, 2020 (https://www.behindthename.com/name/simon-1).

profession! I love how Jesus took Simon's heart, his willingness to listen and absorb what was being taught, and added to his name, Peter (Matthew 16:13–18). Jesus called Simon to follow after Him, to be His disciple and a fisher of men, maybe because of that inner drive He saw in Simon to be a good listener.

Because of a life-altering decision Simon took—to declare what he heard from God to be truth, this good fisherman, Simon, became Simon Peter. Peter means "stone."[12] Though Jesus is the Rock, He used Peter to form the foundation of His church. What an amazing blessing that must have been, tied to a pretty fantastic name change.

Finally, let's look at Saul, a devout Jewish leader. He was passionate and determined. The name Saul means to ask/question,[13] or "asked for/prayed for."[14] I'm going to add that there's deeper meaning to his name, too, since Jesus gave him a new name after Saul's holy encounter on the road to Damascus (Acts 9:3–9).

Perhaps Saul was such an effective leader in the Jewish religion because of his persistent drive to ask questions, study, and apply the knowledge he sought after. The passion he'd developed through study is likely why he terrorized early Christians, who'd been going against everything Saul grew up reading and believing.

Maybe Jesus met with him that day on the road to Damascus because He saw something unique in Saul. Jesus gave Saul the new name Paul, which means "small" or "humble."[15] Though the trait of being a passionate questioner has potential for good, applying this to a man with a humble heart is that much more powerful. Powerful in God's Kingdom, anyway.

After his Damascus road experience, his heart became humble enough that he could hear and see Jesus. But he remained knowledgeable enough to refute errors in judgment and thinking he perceived in those around him. This would have been crucial for

---

[12] "Peter," *Behind the Name*. Date of Access: August 22, 2020 (https://www.behindthename.com/name/peter).

[13] "Saul (given name)," *Wikipedia*. Date of Access: August 10, 2020 (https://en.wikipedia.org/w/index.php?title=Saul_(given_name)&oldid=929995722).

[14] "Saul," *Behind the Name*. Date of Access: August 22, 2020 (https://www.behindthename.com/name/saul).

[15] "Paul," *Behind the Name*. Date of Access: August 22, 2020 (https://www.behindthename.com/paul).

the early church, after Jesus returned to heaven and misinformation began to infiltrate and spread with ease.

To summarize, Jacob was deliberate. He grew up knowing his name and its origin, and his character was tied tightly to his name in a negative way—until he wrestled with God and received grace and favour. After that, a whole nation, blessed by God, grew up from his lineage. Bam! New life, new name.

Simon was good. He had a solid name. Jesus spoke blessing over his life because of his faith, taking him further than he'd have gone alone. He was given a dynamic new name to add to the already solid one he had. He grew to become a church leader and witness of Jesus as Lord. Bam! New life, new name.

Saul was passionate. His name influenced his studies, but hindered him from knowing and seeing God's prophetic promises coming to fruition through Jesus. He was missing out, big time, not to mention traumatizing the early church. Jesus stopped him in his literal tracks and called him out on his misled pursuits. God infused humility into his spirit and used Paul to greatly teach and influence generations to come. Bam! New life, new name.

It appears that something beautiful happens in God's redemption stories when we let go not only of our past mistakes and failures, but also our tendencies and mindsets, and fully embrace the new name He gives us as His sons and daughters.

If it can be said that my name and my worth, in my earlier years, were tied to the idea of being not quite good enough, it should be said that in living this new life, I can now define myself by my new name and true identity: Beloved.

Why Beloved? There's a huge contrast between the two ideas of striving to succeed and knowing you don't have to. My self-assigned name, Not Quite, stands in stark contrast to Beloved when I understand that who I am isn't tied to how much I can do.

Instead, when I know that I am Beloved, everything I do falls under this new umbrella of *already good enough* and *relentlessly loved*. My heart can rest easy as I pursue that which I know is good and right and true.

When we change the way we look at ourselves and what we call ourselves, we change the way we live. Oftentimes I still find myself talking negatively to myself—with a sigh and "Ah, Sara! Come on…!" Those harsh tones stir up frustration that's tied to the idea of messing up or failing. They lead to feelings of unrest that don't need to be there.

To extend the metaphor, there are some key differences between the identities of Not Quite and Beloved. Reflecting on these differences allows me to be more aware of them and the impact they have on my life. From this place of better insight, I can hopefully grow more fully into being Beloved.

Not Quite is still trying to make it to Good Enough. She's aware of every shortfall along the way, and those shortfalls cripple her every step. This creates a heavy burden, though she may not realize it in the middle of her striving. Beloved knows that she's already good enough in the eyes of her Father, because of Jesus's gift of redeemed life through His sacrifice on the cross and His resurrection.

Not Quite is cognizant of others' critiques and criticisms, which often leave her feeling defeated and in despair. Beloved knows she's free, and can allow others their opinions without them affecting her emotions, joy, or overall outlook.

Not Quite lives from a place of constantly striving for achievements that don't satisfy. Beloved can labour and trust that the fruit of her labour will be enough despite the immediate result. That trust offers satisfaction and rest that refreshes, redeems, and readies her for more.

Oh precious Not Quite, your intentions were most often good. They grew out of wanting the best for yourself, for God, and for others. Had you known that being Beloved was truly good enough, you would have suffered so much less heartache along the way.

I leave you, precious Not Quite, with a loving embrace in order to step more fully into Beloved, wherein my heart can thrive.

The Princess reached up
So aware of her dearth
Ashamed

But Abba grabbed hold of her hands
Tenderly
And opened them, palms up
Into His own

He caressed the callouses
And the Princess watched
Again in awe

As the bitter wounds disappeared

Her damaged hands now shone
Radiantly

And she smiled at her Abba
Fully known
Fully loved

No more defined by her wounds
She was free to live
Free to be
The Princess He'd created her to be

A song formed from deep within
A new song

And the Princess pirouetted
Dancing in delight

Intent to live here
Abundant and free
In the shelter of Abba's Kingdom

Fifteen:
Grace, Grace, and More Grace

Since grace is a concept I didn't understand in my earlier years, it has become important to me to reread and study the Scriptures with fresh eyes. I once knew many verses by memorization, but now I've needed to look them up in different translations, to slow down my brain and allow my heart to soak up the words rather than skim over them.

What an exciting exploration this has been! I feel like a brand-new person reading a love letter from God for the very first time!

Growing up, I often struggled to read and meditate on Paul's letters because I felt an air of pompous pride in his words. Maybe that's a ridiculous thought, but it annoyed me that he came across as being so perfect.

How is it that he had everything so darn figured out? I thought. *Did he not struggle at all?*

Paul's writings are the portion of Scripture most littered with the beautiful concept of grace, and he is the one who dug deep to unearth this treasure for us as readers. When I decided to read Paul's letters in different translations, I was finally able to witness the treasure of grace for myself. More so, I was able to release Paul from the chains I'd bound him in with my negative mindset and assumptions.

I came to realize that he certainly did struggle. He was human. Yet his foundation of faith was secure, and he knew how to direct his thoughts and settle his heart in truth. Instead of coming across as off-putting, Paul and his writings became inspirational for me, and I'm thankful for that.

Pondering Paul's writings, I began to see that I was in need of the grace he spoke of—more than I ever realized. I'd grown up aiming to be good enough, but on my own strength. Despite my good intentions, I had missed the message of the gospel altogether.

This realization shocked me for a time. My childhood had been built around church and faith, my youth structured around study and application of the Bible. I'd surrendered my life and dreams to Jesus early on, yearning to know and follow Him. How could I have been so blind to the grace that was core to His message?

DC Talk was a favourite band of mine as a teenager. One of their songs was a catchy tune about so many people learning life lessons the hard way.[16] Singing along passionately, I didn't think of myself as one of those people, and maybe even piously raised myself above them in my naïve, youthful stance that I had things all figured out.

Oh those poor souls, I'd lament. *They're off making bad choices, choosing selfishness before they reach the understanding of the salvation that will transform them.*

Alas, I was the very character in the song, unbeknownst to my determined young heart. I had to learn about grace the hard way. I had to slip off into the deep end of despair and depression to finally understand the message of the gospel that saves and transforms. What a thought!

Oftentimes when reading the Bible, I'll still sit and marvel at the idea of grace. How can God love me so much to give me gifts I don't deserve? Gifts of family, friendships, fulfilled dreams, a truly abundant life… doesn't He realize how much of a train wreck I am? Doesn't He see the physical scars and flaws, especially the heart ones, and shake His head with dismissal?

---

[16] DC Talk, "The Hard Way," *Free at Last*, 1992.

He should. But He doesn't. It's mind-boggling! Especially for someone like me, someone who readily thinks, analyzes, and over-analyzes her world.

God's character offers me comfort: *"For My thoughts are not your thoughts, nor are your ways My ways"* (Isaiah 55:8, NKJV).

Phew! That's a relief! But it's also hard to grasp, apart from choosing to rest from the analysis and simply accept the words at face value. As I practice this more, I realize that this intentional decision is faith in action—faith that God is bigger than my limited understanding, faith that my competence can get me only so far, but His love can take me further. Infinitely further.

I want to unearth and share with you some of the treasures of grace that are written in Scripture. This first verse came alive for me when I compared the following two translations:

From his abundance we have all received one gracious blessing after another. For the law was given through Moses, but God's unfailing love and faithfulness came through Jesus Christ. (John 1:16–17, NLT)

For from his fullness we have all received, grace upon grace. For the law was given through Moses; grace and truth came through Jesus Christ. (John 1:16–17, ESV)

Grace and truth are linked to unfailing love and faithfulness, and this enhances for me the beauty of grace. God's grace and truth, His unfailing love and faithfulness, are offered to me and fulfilled through Jesus Christ—unfailing love despite my many mistakes, faithfulness despite how short I fall time and time again.

Through him [Jesus] we have also obtained access by faith[a] into this grace in which we stand, and we rejoice in hope of the glory of God. (Romans 5:2, ESV)

Grace is accessed by faith alone, and it allows me to hope in the glory of God. What does that hope mean? On a broad scale, the hope of God's glory means that this world is not our home, not our final destination. All the hardships found in our world are a result of sin, but sin has been defeated and conquered, and soon enough we will see the evidence of it—when Jesus calls us home.

More immediately, in each circumstance I walk through, I can breathe peacefully, tread confidently, and press on joyfully because of the hope of God's glory, which is alive, present, and evident in my life. Part of God's glory is Jesus's sacrifice on the cross, and part of Jesus's gift was the Holy Spirit to dwell within us. We are not alone in our trials. We are not hidden amidst the darkness that surrounds us. We are seen, loved, and given all we need in order to overcome. Because of grace.

And now I entrust you to God and the message of his grace that is able to build you up and give you an inheritance with all those he has set apart for himself. (Acts 20:32, NLT)

God's grace indeed transforms us. It builds us up and prepares us for the glorious inheritance yet to come. We see God's power all the more as we surrender our efforts to strive. We become overwhelmed with His majesty when we let down our own crowns of success. We become fulfilled by His love for us when we rest in the satisfaction of who He is and who He says we are, because of grace.

You then, my child, be strengthened by the grace that is in Christ Jesus... (2 Timothy 2:1, ESV)

Paul's charge for Timothy is that he would be strengthened by grace. Timothy was called to leadership, to teaching and preaching the gospel.

I can't imagine it was an easy world to live in during the time of the early church and Roman occupation. But grace isn't just a "Bible word"; it's a powerful, freeing, and literally life-changing concept! Paul knew it had the power to strengthen hearts and transform lives. He knew that for Timothy to be successful at running the race set before him, he needed to be strengthened by grace.

When I'm exhausted from the struggles of striving, when I'm weary from the daily grind, I can choose to accept and rest in the message of grace, and be strengthened. When I remember that a good life is not just about me and what I can do, but actually all about Jesus and what He did on the cross for me, that lifts me into joy rather than sinking me into despair.

Life. Joy. Peace. Purpose. Hope. They are founded on grace, a freely offered gift by the all-knowing, all-powerful God who loves us. Choose grace, and be strengthened.

The Princess was free indeed
Prone to stumbles
But settled
In Abba's tender care

She finished her days
Picking wildflowers once more
Dancing in rain storms
Chasing after butterflies

Aware of the thorns
And muck
And rubble

Free to love and be loved
Free to live
And point others to this same
Abundant Life

This epic wonder of living
So incongruent with the plethora of troubles abounding

Now, then, maybe fairy tales
And happily ever afters
Do come true after all…

Sixteen: Living Good Enough

Looking back on the effect of taking Jesus's words in Matthew 5:48 so literally at such a young age, I'm reminded to dig deeper into the Word. If I really want to know, live, and be changed by the Scriptures, I cannot stop at my first impression of them. Herein lies a battle and a choice: to opt for my own assurance of "smarts" or to eagerly, humbly, and joyfully seek after wisdom that will engulf me in God's marvellous gospel of grace.

I looked up Matthew 5:48 in the Amplified translation of the Bible, and here is what is written:

> *You, therefore, will be perfect [growing into spiritual maturity both in mind and character, actively integrating godly values into your daily life], as your heavenly Father is perfect.* (Matthew 5:48, AMP)

Um, where was this translation when I was growing up? Right there, I guess. Of course. But I didn't see it…

Not stopping here, I looked up the verse in the IVP New Testament Commentary, and here's what it says:

> What Jesus illustrated with graphic, concrete examples earlier in the sermon (vv. 21–47) he now epitomizes in a summary statement that forces us to go beyond mere examples. We can appeal to no law to tell us that we are righteous enough—that would be legalism. Instead, we must desire God's will so much that we seek to please him in every area of our lives—that is holiness. Jesus says that God's law was never about mere rules; instead, God desires a complete righteousness of the heart, a total devotion to God's purposes in this world.
>
> That God becomes the standard of comparison suggests that Jesus' instruction here is exhortation, setting a goal, not assuming a state to which the hearers have already come. (The issue of whether any Christian is perfect is irrelevant here. All of us can learn to better reflect God's character; at the same time, God promises us power to overcome any given temptation; and if we can overcome any temptation, we should choose to say no to every temptation.) And as long as God represents the moral standard, none of us has room to boast; all of us must unite as brothers and sisters in need and seek God's kingdom and righteousness with all our hearts.[17]

Wow. That "perfect" standard that captivated my every attention, it's more about "growing into" as I seek after God, through Jesus, since He alone is perfect. His perfection is trustworthy, hope-filled, and unfailingly loving. Because that's just simply who God is. And I like that.

As I begin this new life of walking in the truth that I am *good enough*, a few verses in Philippians have become meaningful references for me. The first:

---

[17] "Jesus Demands that We Be Perfect Like God (5:48)," *Bible Gateway*. Date of Access: August 24, 2020 (https://www.biblegateway.com/resources/ivp-nt/Jesus-Demands-That-We-Be-Perfect-like). From The IVP New Testament Commentary Series by Intervarsity Press.

> *We rely on what Christ Jesus has done for us. We put no confidence in human effort...* (Philippians 3:3, NLT)

When I accept that in Christ Jesus, by grace, I am Beloved and enough, my human effort can sit on the back-burner. My results no longer define me.

I like the way Paul words this, too: *"We put no confidence in human effort."* This doesn't mean that I won't seek to do my best, but rather that, in doing my best, my confidence still comes from grace and not from the outcome. I am who I am all because of grace, and everything good I accomplish is due to God's grace at work in me. This mindset is absolutely fundamental to walking *good enough*.

The second verse that speaks to my *good enough* mission is this:

> *I once thought these things were valuable, but now I consider them worthless because of what Christ has done. Yes, everything else is worthless when compared with the infinite value of knowing Christ Jesus my Lord. For his sake I have discarded everything else, counting it all as garbage, so that I could gain Christ and become one with him. I no longer count on my own righteousness through obeying the law; rather, I become righteous through faith in Christ. For God's way of making us right with himself depends on faith. I want to know Christ and experience the mighty power that raised him from the dead. I want to suffer with him, sharing in his death, so that one way or another I will experience the resurrection from the dead!* (Philippians 3:7–11, NLT)

Oh, Lord, have mercy! I count everything, all of it, as garbage—all of my striving, all of my goals to get far in life on my own strength… is garbage! That's hard to say. Hard, until I understand that it's only when I delight fully in the Lord and not in myself that the desires of my heart will be fulfilled (Psalm 37:4).

Knowing Jesus and becoming one with Him by His finished work on the Cross, that's the ultimate fulfillment of our hearts. For we were created in God's image, to know Him intimately, to love Him, and to walk with Him. It doesn't get any better than that!

Finally, here's the ultimate kicker:

I don't mean to say that I have already achieved these things or that I have already reached perfection. But I press on to possess that perfection for which Christ Jesus first possessed me. (Philippians 3:12, NLT)

I am going to slip up along the way, both with my own markers for success and with my inability to surrender my striving.

I'm far from perfect in my willingness to let go of perfection. Now, isn't that a funny thought? Yet, in Paul's words, I press on to possess that perfection—the perfection of letting go of perfection and resting in grace, that is.

And that, my friends, is the epic answer I've come to while learning to walk this human road in a heart-space of *good enough*. If Jesus Christ loved me enough, the mess I am, that He died to free me from my need to strive for righteousness and perfection on my own merit, then I am *free indeed!*

My journey can become more about pressing on to be all that I was created to be, and therefore less and less about seeking after human standards of perfection. That is a *good enough* life. A blessed and abundant life. And maybe, dare I say, a perfect one?

We've reached the end of the story, though obviously it continues on.
But the question arises, where do we go from here?
I believe we start with a pause, a moment of reflection…

What is stirring in your heart? The God of creation has just unfolded an intricate redemption story across these pages, but in reality He is at work in millions of redemption stories in the lives of all His dearly beloved children. The point is, do we see it? Believe it? And then, what do we do about it?

    I would like to propose an active prayer to draw us closer to God's heart for us and to witness His redemptive work in each of us beyond the pages of this book. Please join me and fill in the blanks on your own as you cry out to the One who loves you with an everlasting, complete, perfect love…

> Father in heaven, awesome God, and gracious King of my heart,
> Thank You for giving me life and for calling me Beloved.
> Have mercy on me, Lord.
> In the middle of my messy, muddled muck,
> I acknowledge that on my own I am not enough.

Forgive me, Lord.

For forgetting these truths about who You are:

_____
_____
_____

For labelling myself with these contradicting titles that aren't from You:

_____
_____
_____

I lay these burdens and struggles at the Cross of Jesus:

_____
_____
_____

You are my Redeemer, the one who lifts me up and sets my feet on solid ground.
You are my firm foundation.
I call to You,
Trusting that You hear me and will answer me
With unfailing love.
Teach me to walk in Your ways
By grace
Through faith in Jesus Christ—
My More than Enough,
My Hope,
My Freedom,
My Victory.
In Jesus's precious, mighty name I pray,
Amen.

Lord, let it be so. Go forth in peace, and be satisfied by grace.